CHAKRAS

SELF-HEALING TO SELF-ESTEEM

NANDI

Made with ♥ on the Notion Press Platform
www.notionpress.com

To all the founding MASTERS of alternative healing, here and beyond

&

To all the flag-bearers of alternative healing, here and beyond

&

To all practitioners of alternative healing, here and beyond

Contents

Contents

Preface

Chakras as energy centers are largely metaphysical, there are many modern scientific concepts that align with and complement the chakra system. The concept of chakras originates from ancient Indian spiritual traditions, particularly in yoga and Tantra, where they are described as energy centers in the body that correspond to various physical, emotional, and spiritual functions.

Research in bioenergy, neuroplasticity, and sound therapy also continues to explore how the mind and body interact through energy, vibration, and consciousness, which could one day provide a clearer scientific understanding of how chakras function within the human experience.

Understanding the chakras in the context of physiological and psychological development and emotional well-being gives us a powerful tool for addressing mental health issues, improving self-awareness, and fostering personal growth.

Financial healing through chakra work is a holistic approach that addresses the energetic, emotional, and mental blocks that can hinder financial success. By balancing and healing each chakra, you can create a stronger connection to your financial energy and improve your relationship with money.

Each chakra plays a vital role in spiritual healing, and by balancing and clearing blockages in these energy centers, you can deepen your connection to your higher self, the divine, and the universe.

This book is all about understanding chakras. Every chapter is comprehensive by itself, so as you keep reading you will notice the points are being repeated.

Even if you just read selected chapters, you will get the intended message, the intention of this book is that you should get the message so that you can find and chart your own path.

The healing procedures and meditation procedures are not explained in detail, different schools healing procedures and meditations is a complete book by itself. Kindly refer to a suitable teacher/book and take it forward as per your requirements.

You, need not practice all the healing or meditation methods mentioned in this book, choose what you can easily practice, once chosen practice it sincerely and in a proper way, with patience and faith you will get favorable results.

This book is for you to seek the truth on your own terms, understanding the mystery of chakras will help you immensely, hence its always upto you, once you have gained clarity from the right understanding.

When in doubt refer to chapters 31(asana and pranayama) and 32(all the 13 body sysytems)

This book is not a quick fix, it only helps you to start your journey, it's the journey of a lifetime, all the best.

Acknowledgements

To all the traditions of YOGA and the new age healing Masters/ Gurus.

To and all the Great Masters/Gurus who have established the healing traditions to heal and empower oneself and others to seek the highest.

Chakra: Religion, Encyclopaedia Britannica

Grimes, John A. (1996). A Concise Dictionary of Indian Philosophy: Sanskrit Terms Defined in English. State University of New York Press.

Lochtefeld, James G. (2002). The Illustrated Encyclopedia of Hinduism: A-M. Rosen Publishing Group.

Jones, Constance; Ryan, James D. (2006). Encyclopedia of Hinduism. Infobase Publishing.

Heilijgers-Seelen, Dory (1992). The system of five cakras in Kubjikāmatatantra

Beer, Robert (2003). The Handbook of Tibetan Buddhist Symbols. Serindia Publications.

Helena Petrovna Blavatsky, Collected Writings vol. XII (Wheaton, IL: Theosophical Publishing House, 1980)

Mallory, J.P.; Adams, D.Q. (1997). Encyclopedia of Indo-European culture (1 ed.).

Staal, Frits (2008). Discovering the Vedas: Origins, Mantras, Rituals, Insights. Penguin Books.

Collins, Steven (1998). Nirvana and Other Buddhist Felicities. Cambridge University Press.

Edgerton, Franklin (1993). Buddhist Hybrid Sanskrit Grammar and Dictionary (Repr ed.). Delhi: Motilal Banarsidass.

von Glasenapp, Helmuth (1925). Jainism: An Indian Religion of Salvation. Motilal Banarsidass.

White, David Gordon (2001). Tantra in Practice. Motilal Banarsidass.

White, David Gordon (2006). Kiss of the Yogini: "Tantric Sex" in its South Asian Contexts. University of Chicago Press.

Feuerstein, Georg (1998). Tantra: Path of Ecstasy. Shambhala Publications.

Flood, Gavin D. (1996). An Introduction to Hinduism. Cambridge University Press.

White, David Gordon. Yoga in Practice. Princeton University Press 2012,

Trish O'Sullivan (2010), Chakras. In: D.A. Leeming, K. Madden, S. Marlan (eds.), Encyclopedia of Psychology and Religion, Springer Science + Business Media.

Flood, Gavin D. (1996). An Introduction to Hinduism. Cambridge University Press.

Padoux, Andre (2013). The Heart of the Yogini: The Yoginihrdaya, a Sanskrit Tantric Treatise. Oxford University Press.

Pradhan, Basant (2014). Yoga and Mindfulness Based Cognitive Therapy: A Clinical Guide. Springer Verlag.

Sharma, Arvind (2006). A Primal Perspective on the Philosophy of Religion. Springer Verlag.

Müller, Friedrich Max (1899). The Six Systems of Indian Philosophy. Longmans.

Klostermaier, Klaus K. (2010). A Survey of Hinduism (Third ed.). State University of New York Press.

Harvey, Peter (2013). An Introduction to Buddhism: Teachings, History and Practices, 2nd Edition. Cambridge University Press.

Mayer, E. A.; Saper, C. B. (2000). The Biological Basis for Mind Body Interactions. Elsevier.

Wilke, Annette; Moebus, Oliver (2011). Sound and Communication: An Aesthetic Cultural History of Sanskrit Hinduism. Walter de Gruyter.

Johnston, Jay (2010). Elizabeth Burns Coleman and Kevin White (ed.). Medicine, Religion, and the Body. Brill.

Göttler, Christine; Neuber, Wolfgang (2008). Spirits Unseen: The Representation of Subtle Bodies in Early Modern European Culture. Brill Publishers.

Samuel, Geoffrey; Johnston, Jay (2013). Religion and the Subtle

Body in Asia and the West: Between Mind and Body. Routledge.

Bryant, Edwin Francis (2009). The Yoga sūtras of Patañjali: a new edition, translation, and commentary with insights from the traditional commentators. North Point Press.

Syman, Stefanie (2010). The Subtle Body: The Story of Yoga in America. Farrar, Straus and Giroux.

Samuel, Geoffrey; Johnston, Jay (2013). Religion and the Subtle Body in Asia and the West: Between Mind and Body. Routledge.

Snodgrass, Adrian (1992). The Symbolism of the Stupa. Motilal Banarsidass.

Johari, Harish (2000). Chakras: Energy Centers of Transformation. Inner Traditions.

McDaniel, June (2004). Offering Flowers, Feeding Skulls: Popular Goddess Worship in West Bengal. Oxford University Press.

Pott, Philipp H. (2013). Yoga and Yantra: Their Interrelation and Their Significance for Indian Archaeology. Springer Verlag. pp. 8–12. ISBN 978-94-017-5868-0.

Huntington, John C.; Bangdel, Dina (2003). The Circle of Bliss: Buddhist Meditational Art. Serindia Publications. pp. 232–233. ISBN 978-1932476019.

Olson, Carl (2009). Historical Dictionary of Buddhism. Scarecrow Press.

Samuel, Geoffrey; Johnston, Jay (2013). Religion and the Subtle Body in Asia and the West: Between Mind and Body. Routledge.

Mackenzie, Rory (2007). New Buddhist Movements in Thailand: Towards an Understanding of Wat Phra Dhammakaya and Santi Asoke. Routledge.

John C. Huntington, Dina Bangdel, The Circle of Bliss: Buddhist Meditational Art, Serindia Publications, Inc., 2003,

Gyatso, Geshe Kelsang (2014). Clear Light of Bliss : Tantric Meditation Manual. Cumbria, England: Tharpa Publications. Channels, Winds and Drops. ISBN 978-1-910368-03-9 Samuel, Geoffrey; Johnston, Jay (2013). Religion and the Subtle Body in Asia and the West: Between Mind and Body. Routledge.

Rinpoche, Tenzin Wangyal (2002). Mark Dahlby (ed.). Healing

with Form, Energy, and Light: The Five Elements in Tibetan Shamanism, Tantra, and Dzogchen. Ithaca, NY: Snow Lion.

Leland, Kurt (2017). "The Rainbow Body: How the Western Chakra System Came to Be". Quest Magazine. 105 (2 (Spring 2017)). Theosophical Society in America: 25–29.

Samuel, Geoffrey; Johnston, Jay (2013). Religion and the Subtle Body in Asia and the West: Between Mind and Body. Routledge.

Flood, Gavin (2006). The Tantric Body: The Secret Tradition of Hindu Religion. I.B.Tauris.

White, David Gordon (2003). Kiss of the Yogini. Chicago: University of Chicago Press.

Banerjea, Akshaya Kumar (1983). Philosophy of Gorakhnath with Goraksha-Vacana-Sangraha. Motilal Banarsidass.

Samuel, Geoffrey; Johnston, Jay (2013). Religion and the Subtle Body in Asia and the West: Between Mind and Body. Routledge.

Brown, C. Mackenzie (1998). The Devī Gītā: the Song of the Goddess: a translation, annotation, and commentary. Albany (N.Y.): State university of New York press.

Tigunait, Rajmani (1999). Tantra Unveiled: Seducing the Forces of Matter & Spirit. Himalayan Institute Press.

Mumford, John (1988). Ecstasy Through Tantra (Third ed.). Llewellyn Worldwide.

Mindell, Arnold; Sternback-Scott, Sisa; Goodman, Becky (1984). Dreambody: the body's rôle in revealing the self. Taylor & Francis.

Leadbeater, Charles Webster (1972) [1927]. The Chakras. Theosophical Publishing House. ISBN 978-0-8356-0422-2.

Leland, Kurt (2016). Rainbow body : a history of the western chakra system from Blavatsky to Brennan. Lake Worth, Florida: Ibis Press. ISBN 978-0-89254-219-2. OCLC 945949596.

Woodroffe, Sir John (2000). The Serpent Power. Dover Publications. pp. 317ff. ISBN 978-0486230580.

Gardiner, Philip; Osborn, Gary (2006). The Shining Ones: the world's most powerful secret society revealed (Revised and updated ed.). London: Watkins. ISBN 1-84293-150-4.

Judith, Anodea (1999). Wheels of Life: A User's Guide to the

Chakra System. Llewellyn Publications. ISBN 9780875423203.

"John Van Auken : Mysticism - Interpretating the Revelation". Edgarcayce.org. Archived from the original on 26 May 2012.

Sturgess, Stephen (1997). The Yoga Book: a practical guide to self-realization. Rockport, Massachusetts: Element Books. ISBN 1-85230-972-5.

"Archeosophical Society - founded by Tommaso Palamidessi". www.archeosofica.org. Archived from the original on 4 March 2012.

"Myss Library: Chakras". Myss.

Blavatsky, Helena (1892). Theosophical Glossary. Krotona.

Neff, Dio Urmilla (1985). "The Great Chakra Controversy". Yoga Journal (November–December 1985):

"GA010: Chapter I: The Astral Centers". Fremont, Michigan. Retrieved 5 March 2015.

"Contents - GA 10. Initiation and Its Results (1909) - Rudolf Steiner Archive".

"GA010: Initiation and Its Results". Fremont, Michigan. Retrieved 5 March 2015.

Rudolf Steiner, How to Know Higher Worlds

Lowndes, Florin (2000). Enlivening the Chakra of the Heart: The Fundamental Spiritual Exercises of Rudolf Steiner (2nd ed.). London: Sophia Books. ISBN 1-85584-053-7.

"Chakras". Edinburgh Skeptics Society. 17 January 2019. Retrieved 9 February 2021.

Further reading

Apte, Vaman Shivram (1965). The Practical Sanskrit Dictionary (fourth revised & enlarged ed.). Delhi: Motilal Banarsidass. ISBN 81-208-0567-4.

Bucknell, Roderick; Stuart-Fox, Martin (1986). The Twilight Language: Explorations in Buddhist Meditation and Symbolism. London: Curzon Press. ISBN 0-312-82540-4.

Edgerton, Franklin (2004) [1953]. Buddhist Hybrid Sanskrit Grammar and Dictionary (Reprint ed.). Delhi: Motilal Banarsidass Publishers. ISBN 81-208-0999-8. (Two volumes)

Flood, Gavin (1996). An Introduction to Hinduism. Cambridge: Cambridge University Press. ISBN 0-521-43878-0.

Chia, Mantak; Chia, Maneewan (1993). Awaken Healing Light of the Tao. Healing Tao Books.

Dale, Cyndi (2009). The Subtle Body: An Encyclopedia of Your Energetic Anatomy. Boulder, Colorado: Sounds True. ISBN 978-1-59179-671-8.

Monier-Williams, Monier. A Sanskrit-English Dictionary. Delhi: Motilal Banarsidass.

Prabhananda, S. (2000). Studies on the Tantras (Second reprint ed.). Calcutta: The Ramakrishna Mission Institute of Culture. ISBN 81-85843-36-8.

Rinpoche, Tenzin Wangyal (2002). Healing with Form, Energy, and Light. Ithaca, New York: Snow Lion Publications. ISBN 1-55939-176-6.

Saraswati, Swami Sivananda (1953–2001). Kundalini Yoga. Tehri-Garhwal, India: Divine Life Society. foldout chart. ISBN 81-7052-052-5.

Tulku, Tarthang (2007). Tibetan Relaxation. The illustrated guide to Kum Nye massage and movement – A yoga from the Tibetan tradition. London: Dunkan Baird Publishers. ISBN 978-1-84483-404-4.

Woodroffe, John (1964) [1919]. The Serpent Power. Madras, India: Ganesh & Co. ISBN 0-486-23058-9.

Banerji, S. C. Tantra in Bengal. Second Revised and Enlarged Edition. (Manohar: Delhi, 1992) ISBN 81-85425-63-9

Saraswati, Swami Sivananda (1953–2001). Kundalini Yoga. Divine Life Society. ISBN 81-7052-052-5.

Goswami, Shyam Sundar. Layayoga: The Definitive Guide to the Chakras and Kundalini, Routledge & Kegan Paul, 1980.

Sharp, Michael (2005). Dossier of the Ascension: A Practical Guide to Chakra Activation and Kundalini Awakening (1st ed.). Avatar Publications. ISBN 0-9735379-3-0. Khalsa, Guru Dharam Singh; O'Keeffe, Darryl. The Kundalini Yoga Experience Simon & Schuster, 2002.

Judith, Anodea (1996). Eastern Body Western Mind: Psychology and the Chakra System As A Path to the Self. Berkeley, California, USA: Celestial Arts Publishing. ISBN 0-89087-815-3

Lowndes, Florin. 'Enlivening the Chakra of the Heart: The Fundamental Spiritual Exercises of Rudolf Steiner' ISBN 1-85584-053-7, first English edition 1998 from the original German edition of 1996, comparing 'traditional' chakra teaching, and that of C.W. Leadbeater, with that of Rudolf Steiner.

Any individual or publisher who feels his or her name has to be included in the acknowledgements, kindly contact me and I will do the needful.

CHAPTER I

CHAKRAS

According to various spiritual and healing traditions, chakras are energy centers in the body, especially in Hinduism and Buddhism. The word "chakra" comes from the Sanskrit term meaning "wheel" or "disk," representing spinning vortexes of energy. There are seven main chakras, each associated with different aspects of life, emotions, and physical well-being.

Chakras offer an integrated approach to understanding how the mind, body, and spirit work together to maintain health and well-being.

Chakras are energy centers within the body that regulate the flow of life force energy (prana, chi, etc.). When a chakra is blocked or imbalanced, it can manifest as physical illness, emotional distress, or spiritual stagnation.

By maintaining balance in the chakras, we support optimal physiological functioning, emotional health, and spiritual growth.

1) **Root Chakra (Muladhara)**

Location: Base of the spine, near the tailbone

Color: Red

Element: Earth

Function: Grounding, security, survival, and stability

Imbalance Symptoms: Fear, anxiety, insecurity, and financial instability

2) **Sacral Chakra (Svadhisthana)**

Location: Lower abdomen, about 2 inches below the navel closer to the reproductive organs

Color: Orange

Element: Water

Function: Creativity, sexuality, pleasure, and emotional balance

Imbalance Symptoms: Emotional instability, sexual dysfunction, lack of creativity

3) **Solar Plexus Chakra (Manipura)**

Location: Upper abdomen, around the stomach area

Color: Yellow

Element: Fire

Function: Personal power, confidence, and self-esteem

Imbalance Symptoms: Low self-esteem, lack of direction, anger issues

4) Heart Chakra (Anahata)

Location: Center of the chest, near the heart

Color: Green or Pink

Element: Air

Function: Love, compassion, empathy, and relationships

Imbalance Symptoms: Difficulty with relationships, loneliness, emotional pain

5) Throat Chakra (Vishuddha)

Location: Throat region

Color: Blue

Element: Ether (space)

Function: Communication, self-expression, and truth

Imbalance Symptoms: Difficulty speaking up, fear of speaking, sore throat

6) **Third Eye Chakra (Ajna)**

Location: Forehead, between the eyebrows

Color: Indigo

Element: Light

Function: Intuition, insight, wisdom, and psychic abilities

Imbalance Symptoms: Lack of clarity, poor decision-making, inability to trust intuition

7) Crown Chakra (Sahasrara)

Location: Top of the head

Color: Violet or white

Element: Thought

Function: Spirituality, connection to the divine, enlightenment

Imbalance Symptoms: Spiritual disconnection, lack of purpose, closed-mindedness

CHAPTER II

CHAKRAS BALANCING

1. Root Chakra (Muḷadhara)

Element: Earth

Affirmation: "I am safe and secure."

Location: Base of spine, near the tailbone

Signs of Imbalance:

Feeling unsafe or insecure

Financial instability

Fearfulness or anxiety

Physical issues: lower back pain, leg pain, or fatigue

How to Balance:

Yoga Poses: Mountain Pose, Tree Pose, Warrior Pose

Crystals: Red jasper, hematite, black tourmaline

Essential Oils: Cedarwood, patchouli, sandalwood

Activities: Walking barefoot on grass, gardening, or grounding meditation

2. Sacral Chakra (Svadhisthana)

Element: Water

Affirmation: "I am creative."

Location: Lower abdomen, 2 inches below the navel closer to reproductive organ

Signs of Imbalance:

Difficulty expressing emotions or creativity

Feelings of guilt or shame, especially around pleasure

Sexual dysfunction or lack of passion

Physical issues: reproductive or urinary problems

How to Balance:

Yoga Poses: Cobra Pose, Goddess Pose

Crystals: Carnelian, orange calcite, moonstone

Essential Oils: Ylang-ylang, jasmine, clary sage

Activities: Dancing, swimming, or indulging in a creative hobby

3. Solar Plexus Chakra (Manipura)

Element: Fire

Affirmation: "I am confident in my life."

Location: Upper abdomen, near the stomach

Signs of Imbalance:

Low self-esteem or feelings of helplessness

Aggression or controlling tendencies

Digestive issues, ulcers, or fatigue

How to Balance:

Yoga Poses: Boat Pose, Warrior III

Crystals: Citrine, tiger's eye, yellow calcite

Essential Oils: Lemon, ginger, peppermint

Activities: Journaling personal goals, sunbathing, or core-strengthening exercises

4. Heart Chakra (Anahata)

Element: Air

Affirmation: "I am lovingly connected to all."

Location: Center of the chest

Signs of Imbalance:

Struggles in relationships or difficulty forgiving

Jealousy, bitterness, or emotional withdrawal

Physical issues: heart problems, upper back pain

How to Balance:

Yoga Poses: Bridge Pose, Cow Face Pose

Crystals: Rose quartz, green aventurine, jade

Essential Oils: Rose, lavender

Activities: Practicing gratitude, volunteering, or spending time in nature

5. Throat Chakra (Vishuddha)

Element: Ether (space)

Affirmation: "I speak with clarity and confidence."

Location: Throat

Signs of Imbalance:

Difficulty expressing thoughts or being misunderstood

Gossiping, lying, or excessive quietness

Physical issues: sore throat, neck pain, or thyroid problems
How to Balance:
Yoga Poses: Fish Pose, Shoulder Stand, Lion's Pose
Crystals: Aquamarine, blue lace agate, turquoise
Essential Oils: Chamomile, frankincense
Activities: Singing, chanting, or practicing active listening

6. Third Eye Chakra (Ajna)

Element: Light
Affirmation: "I trust my intuition."
Location: Between the eyebrows
Signs of Imbalance:
Lack of intuition, indecision, or overthinking
Difficulty concentrating or feeling disconnected
Physical issues: headaches, eye strain, or sleep disturbances
How to Balance:
Yoga Poses: Child's Pose, Forward Fold
Crystals: Amethyst, lapis lazuli, fluorite
Essential Oils: Lavender, sandalwood, clary sage
Activities: Meditation, dream journaling, or visualization exercises

7. Crown Chakra (Sahasrara)

Element: Thought (or Spirit)
Affirmation: "I am connected to the divine."
Location: Top of the head
Signs of Imbalance:
Feeling disconnected from spirituality or lacking purpose
Closed-mindedness or overattachment to material things
Physical issues: migraines, depression, or fatigue
How to Balance:
Yoga Poses: Corpse Pose, Lotus Pose
Crystals: Clear quartz, selenite, diamond
Essential Oils: Frankincense, myrrh, lotus
Activities: Silent meditation, prayer, or spending time under the stars

CHAPTER III

CHAKRA IMBALANCES

A lack of energy often has a profound connection to imbalances in the chakras, the body's energy centers. Each chakra plays a role in how energy flows through your physical, emotional, and spiritual systems. When one or more chakras are blocked or underactive, it can result in fatigue, lethargy, or a sense of being "stuck." Here's a deep dive into how each chakra relates to energy levels, why imbalances happen, and how to restore vitality.

1. Root Chakra (Muladhara): Energy Foundation

Connection to Energy: The root chakra anchors you to Earth's energy, providing a sense of stability and physical vitality. A blocked root chakra leads to feelings of insecurity and physical exhaustion.

Signs of Imbalance:

Chronic fatigue or weakness

Anxiety and restlessness

Financial or physical instability

Causes:

Unresolved survival fears (money, shelter, health)

Disconnection from nature or physical activity

Restoration Practices:

Grounding exercises like walking barefoot on soil

Eating root vegetables (carrots, potatoes)

Affirmation: "I am grounded, safe, and supported."

2. Sacral Chakra (Svadhisthana): Emotional Energy

Connection to Energy: This chakra governs emotional energy, creativity, and pleasure. An imbalance can cause emotional exhaustion or apathy.

Signs of Imbalance:

Lack of enthusiasm or joy

Feeling uninspired or "numb"

Reproductive or lower abdominal issues

Causes:

Repressed emotions or creativity

Guilt or shame from past actions

Restoration Practices:

Water therapy: baths, swimming, or visualizing flowing water

Creative activities like painting or dancing

Affirmation: "I embrace my emotions and creativity freely."

3. Solar Plexus Chakra (Manipura): Personal Power

Connection to Energy: The solar plexus fuels physical energy and willpower. When blocked, it results in low motivation and a sense of powerlessness.

Signs of Imbalance:

Procrastination or lack of direction

Digestive issues

Overwhelm or burnout from overexertion

Causes:

Self-doubt or fear of failure

Overworking without rest

Restoration Practices:

Sunlight exposure (solar energy)

Breath of fire (similar to kapalbathi but rapid)

Affirmation: "I am confident, strong, and full of energy."

4. Heart Chakra (Anahata): Emotional Vitality

Connection to Energy: The heart chakra fuels emotional resilience and compassion. Blockages here lead to emotional fatigue or feelings of isolation.

Signs of Imbalance:

Lack of empathy or connection with others

Physical fatigue, especially in the chest or upper body

Holding onto grudges or past heartbreaks

Causes:

Unforgiveness or unresolved grief

Isolation or lack of self-love

Restoration Practices:

Loving-kindness meditation (Metta)

Heart-opening yoga poses (Camel Pose, Cobra Pose)

Affirmation: "I am open to giving and receiving love."

5. Throat Chakra (Vishuddha): Expressive Energy

Connection to Energy: Governs the energy of communication and expression. Blockages can create mental fatigue and resistance to sharing thoughts.

Signs of Imbalance:

Feeling unheard or unable to express yourself

Chronic throat issues or stiffness in the neck

Mental exhaustion from overthinking

Causes:

Suppressed thoughts or truths

Fear of judgment

Restoration Practices:

Vocal toning or chanting "Ham"

Journaling your thoughts freely

Affirmation: "I express myself with clarity and confidence."

6. Third Eye Chakra (Ajna): Mental Energy

Connection to Energy: Governs mental clarity, intuition, and focus. A blocked third eye leads to brain fog, confusion, and a lack of inspiration.

Signs of Imbalance:

Overthinking or indecisiveness

Headaches or vision problems

Feeling disconnected from intuition

Causes:

Information overload

Ignoring intuitive insights

Restoration Practices:

Visualization exercises (imagine an indigo light on your forehead)

Meditation to calm the mind

Affirmation: "I trust my intuition and inner wisdom."

7. Crown Chakra (Sahasrara): Spiritual Energy

Connection to Energy: Represents your connection to universal energy. Blockages result in spiritual fatigue or feeling "cut off" from purpose.

Signs of Imbalance:

Feeling lost or purposeless

Sleep disturbances

Migraines or pressure in the head

Causes:

Attachment to material concerns

Resistance to spiritual growth

Restoration Practices:

Silence meditation or prayer

Spending time in nature to connect with universal energy

Affirmation: “I am connected to divine energy.”

CHAPTER IV

CHAKRAS MEDITATION

Step-by-Step Basic Meditation

Meditation is a powerful tool for chakra healing, as it helps you connect with your inner energy, clear blockages, and restore balance. Below are detailed meditation practices for each of the seven main chakras, focusing on healing, alignment, and deep emotional connection.

Relax and Center Yourself

Close your eyes and take a few deep breaths.

Inhale through your nose, hold for a moment and exhale slowly through your mouth.

Focus on the present moment, letting go of any distractions.

Start with the Root Chakra (Muladhara) and move upward through Each Chakra,

1.Root Chakra (Muladhara)

Location: Base of the spine.

Focus: Imagine a red glowing sphere or spinning wheel at the base of your spine.

Mantra: Silently chant or say "Lam" (pronounced "lum") while focusing on this chakra.

Visualization: Picture energy rising from the earth, grounding you and providing stability.

Spend 2-5 minutes here before moving on.

Move Upward Through Each Chakra

For each chakra:

2. Sacral Chakra (Svadhisthana):

Location: Below the navel.

Color: Orange.

Mantra: "Vam" (pronounced "vum").

Focus: Flowing energy like water, encouraging creativity and pleasure.

3.Solar Plexus Chakra (Manipura):

Location: Upper abdomen.

Color: Yellow.

Mantra: “Ram” (pronounced “rum”).

Focus: A radiant sun, empowering your confidence and personal strength.

4.Heart Chakra (Anahata):

Location: Center of the chest.

Color: Green or pink.

Mantra: “Yam” (pronounced “yum”).

Focus: A warm, glowing light expanding with love and compassion.

5.Throat Chakra (Vishuddha):

Location: Throat.

Color: Blue.

Mantra: “Ham” (pronounced “hum”).

Focus: A clear blue sky, enabling authentic expression and truth.

6. Third Eye Chakra (Ajna):

Location: Between the eyebrows.

Color: Indigo.

Mantra: “Om” (or “Aum”).

Focus: A glowing indigo light, sharpening intuition and insight.

7.Crown Chakra (Sahasrara):

Location: Top of the head.

Color: Violet or white.

Mantra: Silence or “Om.”

Focus: A lotus flower or a beam of white light connecting you to the universe.

Full-Body Alignment

After visualizing each chakra, imagine all seven spinning harmoniously in alignment.

See energy flowing freely from the base of your spine to the crown of your head.

Closing the Meditation

Slowly bring your awareness back to the room.

Take a few deep breaths and express gratitude for the experience.

Optionally, journal any insights or feelings you experienced during the meditation.

Tips for Deepening Your Practice

Consistency: Practice regularly, 10-15 minutes a day.

Body Awareness: Pay attention to physical sensations or emotions during the meditation, as they may indicate blockages.

Affirmations: Repeat chakra-specific affirmations to strengthen their energy.

Journaling: Reflect on your experiences and track your progress over time.

Step-by-Step Advance Meditation

Meditation is a powerful tool for chakra healing, as it helps you connect with your inner energy, clear blockages, and restore balance. Below are detailed meditation practices for each of the seven main chakras, focusing on healing, alignment, and deep emotional connection.

Relax and Center Yourself

Close your eyes and take a few deep breaths.

Inhale through your nose, hold for a moment and exhale slowly through your mouth.

Focus on the present moment, letting go of any distractions.

1. Root Chakra Meditation (Muladhara)

Purpose: To ground yourself, feel secure, and connect with the earth.

What You Need: A quiet space

Essential oils for the Root Chakra (e.g., Cedarwood, Vetiver, Patchouli)

Comfortable seated position or lying down

Optional: Grounding crystals (e.g., Hematite, Red Jasper)

Steps:

Grounding: Sit comfortably or lie down with your feet firmly on the ground. Imagine roots extending from the base of your spine deep into the earth, anchoring you securely.

Breathing: Take slow, deep breaths. Inhale through your nose, and exhale through your mouth. With each exhale, imagine releasing tension and anxiety, feeling yourself sink deeper into the earth.

Visualization: Visualize a red glowing ball of energy at the base of your spine. See it growing brighter with each breath, expanding throughout your body and grounding you to the earth.

Affirmation: Repeat the affirmation, "I am safe, secure, and supported by the earth."

Deepening Connection: Continue breathing deeply, focusing on the security and stability that the earth provides. Feel a sense of strength and safety filling your entire being.

Duration: 10-15 minutes

2. Sacral Chakra Meditation (Svadhisthana)

Purpose: To unlock creativity, emotional expression, and sensuality.

What You Need: A quiet space

Essential oils for the Sacral Chakra (e.g., Ylang Ylang, Orange, Clary Sage)

Comfortable seated position

Optional: Creativity-enhancing crystals (e.g., Carnelian, Orange Calcite)

Steps:

Relaxation: Sit comfortably with your hands on your lap. Take a few deep breaths to relax and center yourself.

Breathing: Focus on your breath. As you inhale, visualize the vibrant orange glowing ball of light energy entering your lower abdomen. With each exhale, imagine releasing any emotional blockages or negative energy.

Visualization: Imagine a glowing orange ball at your lower abdomen, just below the navel closer to the sexual organ. This light represents your creative energy and emotional well-being. See it expanding with each breath, radiating warmth and creativity.

Affirmation: Repeat the affirmation, "I embrace my emotions and creativity."

Connection: With every breath, feel yourself becoming more open and receptive to creative expression, joyful experiences, and emotional flow.

Duration: 10-15 minutes

3. Solar Plexus Chakra Meditation (Manipura)

Purpose: To build personal power, confidence, and self-esteem.

What You Need: A quiet space

Essential oils for the Solar Plexus Chakra (e.g., Lemon, Ginger, Peppermint)

Comfortable seated position

Optional: Empowering crystals (e.g., Citrine, Tiger's Eye)

Steps:

Relaxation: Sit up straight, relax your shoulders, and take several deep breaths to center yourself.

Breathing: Inhale deeply through your nose, filling your abdomen. Exhale slowly, releasing any feelings of doubt or low energy.

Visualization: Focus on a bright yellow ball of glowing light at your solar plexus (closer to the sexual organ). With each breath, see this ball of light growing larger, shining brighter, and empowering you with confidence and self-belief.

Affirmation: Repeat the affirmation, "I am capable of achieving my goals."

Empowerment: Feel your sense of personal power grow stronger. As the yellow energy expands, visualize yourself radiating confidence, assertiveness, and inner strength.

Duration: 10-15 minutes

4. Heart Chakra Meditation (Anahata)

Purpose: To open your heart to love, compassion, and emotional healing.

What You Need: A quiet space

Essential oils for the Heart Chakra (e.g., Rose, Geranium, Lavender)

Comfortable seated position

Optional: Loving crystals (e.g., Rose Quartz, Green Aventurine)

Steps:

Relaxation: Sit comfortably with your hands over your heart. Close your eyes and take several deep breaths, letting go of any tension.

Breathing: Focus on your breath, inhaling deeply into your chest, filling your heart space with love. Exhale, releasing any negative emotions or emotional blockages.

Visualization: Visualize a glowing green or pink light at your heart center. See this light expanding with each breath, filling your chest with warmth, love, and compassion. Imagine it reaching out to those around you.

Affirmation: Repeat the affirmation, "I am worthy of love. I give and receive love freely."

Healing: As you breathe deeply, feel any emotional wounds healing. Visualize yourself surrounded by unconditional love, healing from past hurts, and opening your heart fully to love and compassion.

Duration: 10-15 minutes

5. Throat Chakra Meditation (Vishuddha)

Purpose: To enhance communication, self-expression, and truth.

What You Need: A quiet space

Essential oils for the Throat Chakra (e.g., Chamomile, Peppermint, Eucalyptus)

Comfortable seated position

Optional: Clear communication crystals (e.g., Blue Lace Agate, Aquamarine)

Steps:

Relaxation: Sit with your spine straight and your shoulders relaxed. Take deep, slow breaths to center your mind.

Breathing: As you inhale, imagine a clear blue light entering your throat. With each exhale, release any feelings of fear, doubt, or suppressed communication.

Visualization: Picture a blue vibrant light at your throat. As you breathe, see this light expanding, allowing you to speak your truth with clarity and confidence.

Affirmation: Repeat the affirmation, "I express myself with clarity and truth."

Expression: Visualize yourself speaking clearly and authentically, sharing your ideas and feelings with confidence and ease.

Duration: 10-15 minutes

6. Third Eye Chakra Meditation (Ajna)

Purpose: To enhance intuition, clarity, and spiritual insight.

What You Need: A quiet space

Essential oils for the Third Eye Chakra (e.g., Frankincense, Lavender, Clary Sage)

Comfortable seated position

Optional: Intuitive crystals (e.g., Amethyst, Lapis Lazuli)

Steps:

Relaxation: Sit in a comfortable position with your spine straight and your hands resting on your knees. Close your eyes and take deep, steady breaths.

Breathing: Focus on your breath, allowing your mind to clear. With each inhale, imagine intuitive energy entering your forehead. With each exhale, release mental clutter or confusion.

Visualization: Visualize a glowing indigo light at your third eye (between your eyebrows). See this light growing brighter with each breath, unlocking your intuition and spiritual insight.

Affirmation: Repeat the affirmation, "I trust my intuition."

Intuitive Connection: With each breath, feel yourself becoming more attuned to your inner wisdom, gaining clarity, insight, and connection to your higher self.

Duration: 10-15 minutes

7. Crown Chakra Meditation (Sahasrara)

Purpose: To connect with divine consciousness, spiritual enlightenment, and universal energy.

What You Need: A quiet and clean space

Essential oils for the Crown Chakra (e.g., Neroli, Lavender, Frankincense)

Comfortable seated position

Optional: Spiritual crystals (e.g., Clear Quartz, Amethyst)

Steps:

Relaxation: Sit comfortably with your spine straight and your hands resting on your lap. Close your eyes and take several deep breaths to relax.

Breathing: Focus on your breath, inhaling deeply through your nose and exhaling through your mouth. With each inhale, imagine divine energy entering the top of your head.

Visualization: Visualize a glowing violet or white light at the top of your head. See this light expanding upward, connecting you to universal consciousness, higher wisdom, and divine energy.

Affirmation: Repeat the affirmation, "I am connected to the divine."

Divine Connection: As you breathe, feel yourself becoming one with the universe, opening your mind and heart to spiritual insight and divine love.

Duration: 10-15 minutes

Guidelines for Deepening, Chakra Meditation Practice:

Consistency: Meditate daily for a minimum of 30 minutes. Consistency will help you achieve deeper healing and connection.

Breathing: Focus on slow, deep, and controlled breathing to enhance the effectiveness of the meditation.

Environment: Create a peaceful environment—dim lighting, calming music, and comfortable seating will help you focus.

Journaling: After each meditation, spend a few moments journaling any thoughts, feelings, or insights that arose during the session.

CHAPTER V

CHAKRAS AND HUMAN EVOLUTION

Everyone is evolving, everything is evolving, even the chakras are evolving.

Chakras and human evolution are deeply interconnected, as the development of chakras mirrors humanity's physical, emotional, mental, and spiritual growth over time. This connection reflects both individual evolution across lifetimes and the collective evolution of humanity as a species.

Chakras and Stages of Human Evolution

1. Root Chakra (Muladhara)

Evolutionary Stage: Survival and physical existence.

Era: Early human history (prehistoric times).

Focus: Primitive humans focused on survival—finding food, shelter, and safety from predators. This corresponds to the root chakra's themes of grounding, stability, and connection to the Earth.

Human Development: Establishing basic security and building the foundation for life.

2. Sacral Chakra (Svadhisthana)

Evolutionary Stage: Reproduction, creativity, and early social structures.

Era: Early tribal societies.

Focus: Humans began forming relationships, exploring sexuality, and creating early forms of art and culture. The sacral chakra governs emotional connections, pleasure, and creativity.

Human Development: Emotional bonding and the beginnings of self-expression.

3. Solar Plexus Chakra (Manipura)

Evolutionary Stage: Personal power, identity, and autonomy.

Era: Agricultural and early civilization periods.

Focus: Humans developed structured societies, laws, and individual roles. The solar plexus chakra reflects the emergence of personal will, self-esteem, and control over the environment.

Human Development: Mastery of resources and the assertion of individual power within a community.

4. Heart Chakra (Anahata)

Evolutionary Stage: Compassion, love, and interconnectedness.

Era: Rise of philosophies, religions, and global connections.

Focus: Humanity began to understand the importance of love, cooperation, and emotional balance. The heart chakra represents the bridge between the physical and spiritual realms, fostering empathy and universal love.

Human Development: Moving beyond survival to create deeper connections with others and the environment.

5. Throat Chakra (Vishuddha)

Evolutionary Stage: Communication, truth, and self-expression.

Era: Industrial and technological revolutions.

Focus: This period saw the rise of communication technologies, global dialogue, and the expression of individuality on a large scale. The throat chakra governs the power of words and authenticity.

Human Development: Sharing ideas, innovating, and expressing personal and collective truths.

6. Third Eye Chakra (Ajna)

Evolutionary Stage: Intuition, insight, and higher wisdom.

Era: Modern and post-modern era.

Focus: As humans explore deeper questions about consciousness and the universe, the third eye chakra guides intuitive understanding and expanded awareness. This aligns with breakthroughs in science, psychology, and spirituality.

Human Development: Seeking answers to life's mysteries and integrating knowledge with intuition.

7. Crown Chakra (Sahasrara)

Evolutionary Stage: Spiritual enlightenment and universal connection.

Era: Future or ascended humanity.

Focus: The crown chakra represents the pinnacle of human evolution—unity with the divine, collective consciousness, and the realization of oneness. This stage reflects humanity's potential for spiritual transcendence.

Human Development: Achieving harmony with all life and universal awareness.

The Spiral of Evolution

Human evolution is not linear; it's a spiral. As individuals and societies grow, they revisit lower chakras from a higher perspective.

For example:

A society focused on technological advancement (Throat Chakra) may need to revisit Root Chakra issues like sustainability.

Individuals exploring spirituality (Crown Chakra) must still ground themselves through the Root Chakra to stay balanced.

Chakras and Collective Awakening

Current Evolution: Humanity is moving from a Solar Plexus Chakra focus (power dynamics, competition) to a Heart Chakra focus (unity, compassion). This transition is evident in global movements for equality, environmental consciousness, and interconnectedness.

Future Evolution: As humanity aligns with the Third Eye and Crown Chakras, collective intuition, wisdom, and spiritual awakening will guide advancements in science, philosophy, and universal understanding.

Chakras as a Map for Individual and Species Growth

Each person mirrors this evolutionary journey in their own life, beginning with survival (Root Chakra) and progressing toward self-realization and spiritual connection (Crown Chakra).

Societies and cultures also reflect these stages, often focusing on the dominant chakra that aligns with their priorities.

CHAPTER VI

CHAKRAS AND AGE

From innocence to wisdom, its an ageing process.

Chakras and age have a fascinating relationship. Throughout life, our chakras develop, evolve, and reflect different stages of growth, experience, and energy flow. Each chakra becomes more prominent or undergoes specific developmental shifts during certain life stages, aligning with our physical, emotional, and spiritual growth.

Chakras and Developmental Stages

1. Root Chakra (Muladhara)

Age Range: Conception to 7 years old.

Focus: Foundation, survival, safety, and grounding.

Developmental Aspects: During early childhood, we focus on building trust, feeling safe, and establishing a secure base in the world. This is the time when we form our basic sense of belonging and connection to family and Earth.

Signs of Imbalance: Childhood trauma, neglect, or insecurity during this stage may lead to root chakra imbalances in adulthood, such as anxiety or instability.

2. Sacral Chakra (Svadhisthana)

Age Range: 8 to 14 years old.

Focus: Creativity, emotions, relationships, and pleasure.

Developmental Aspects: This stage involves exploring emotions, forming relationships, and understanding one's creative and sexual identity. Adolescents become aware of desires and personal boundaries.

Signs of Imbalance: Emotional suppression or overly restrictive environments can block this chakra, leading to difficulties with intimacy and creativity later in life.

3. Solar Plexus Chakra (Manipura)

Age Range: 15 to 21 years old.

Focus: Personal power, confidence, willpower, and self-esteem.

Developmental Aspects: Young adulthood is about establishing independence, discovering one's identity, and building confidence. It's a time to take risks, assert individuality, and develop self-discipline.

Signs of Imbalance: Over-controlling or overly critical environments during this stage may create self-esteem issues or a lack of motivation.

4. Heart Chakra (Anahata)

Age Range: 22 to 35 years old.

Focus: Love, compassion, relationships, and balance.

Developmental Aspects: As adults form deeper relationships and pursue emotional fulfillment, the heart chakra guides connections with others and the balance between giving and receiving love.

Signs of Imbalance: Heartbreak, unresolved grief, or emotional shutdown can block the heart chakra, affecting relationships and self-love.

5. Throat Chakra (Vishuddha)

Age Range: 36 to 42 years old.

Focus: Communication, truth, and self-expression.

Developmental Aspects: This stage focuses on living authentically, speaking one's truth, and refining communication. People seek to align their external expression with their inner values.

Signs of Imbalance: A blocked throat chakra may result from fear of judgment or an inability to express oneself, leading to feelings of frustration or inauthenticity.

6. Third Eye Chakra (Ajna)

Age Range: 43 to 49 years old.

Focus: Intuition, insight, and wisdom.

Developmental Aspects: This period brings a shift toward introspection and deeper understanding. People develop heightened intuition and seek to connect with their inner wisdom and life's bigger picture.

Signs of Imbalance: Over-reliance on logic or ignoring intuition can hinder the third eye chakra, leading to confusion or lack of purpose.

7. Crown Chakra (Sahasrara)

Age Range: 50 years and beyond.

Focus: Spiritual connection, enlightenment, and universal consciousness.

Developmental Aspects: As individuals reflect on their life journey, they often seek a deeper connection with the universe, spirituality, and higher purpose. This is a time for wisdom, transcendence, and understanding the interconnectedness of all life.

Signs of Imbalance: Fear of aging, resistance to change, or lack of spiritual connection can block the crown chakra.

The Chakra Lifecycle

Childhood: Root and Sacral chakras dominate, as physical and emotional foundations are established.

Adolescence to Early Adulthood: Solar Plexus and Heart chakras are more active, shaping identity, relationships, and emotional balance.

Middle Age: Throat and Third Eye chakras begin to lead, promoting self-expression and inner wisdom.

Later Life: Crown chakra takes precedence, focusing on spiritual growth and universal awareness.

Healing Chakras at Different Ages

Early Years (Root Chakra): Emphasize nurturing, safety, and grounding activities like nature walks and family bonding.

Teen Years (Sacral & Solar Plexus Chakras): Encourage creative outlets, self-expression, and confidence-building practices.

Adulthood (Heart & Throat Chakras): Cultivate meaningful relationships, open communication, and alignment with personal values.

Later Life (Third Eye & Crown Chakras): Focus on meditation, spiritual practices, and embracing wisdom and life's purpose.

CHAPTER VII

CHAKRAS - MALE AND FEMALE

The male and female aspects of the 7 chakras reflect the balance of masculine and feminine energies within each energy center. These energies are not necessarily tied to gender, but rather to archetypal qualities such as active (masculine) and receptive (feminine) energies, which exist within all individuals, regardless of gender.

1. Root Chakra (Muladhara) – Grounding, Stability, Security

Masculine Aspect (Active, Protective): The root chakra's masculine energy is about assertiveness, strength, and survival. It embodies the qualities of protection, providing a solid foundation for physical safety and security. This energy is connected to action, like building stability and ensuring survival.

Feminine Aspect (Receptive, Nurturing): The feminine aspect of the root chakra is connected to nurturing, sustenance, and care. It reflects the ability to receive and be supported, fostering a sense of stability by being open to the flow of resources and support. This energy relates to mothering instincts and feeling grounded in the natural world.

2. Sacral Chakra (Svadhisthana) – Creativity, Emotional Flow, Sensuality

Masculine Aspect (Active, Creative Force): The masculine energy of the sacral chakra is about creating and manifesting. It embodies the active, driven energy that initiates creativity, personal expression, and action. This energy is linked to passion and sexual vitality, as well as the willpower to pursue desires.

Feminine Aspect (Receptive, Emotional Fluidity): The feminine energy of the sacral chakra is about fluidity, emotional depth, and nurturing creativity. It is connected to the ability to flow with one's emotions and desires, expressing creativity through sensitivity, intuition, and surrender. The feminine sacral energy embodies sensuality, connection, and the power of emotional bonding.

3. Solar Plexus Chakra (Manipura) – Personal Power, Confidence, Self-Esteem

Masculine Aspect (Active, Assertive Power): The masculine energy of the solar plexus chakra is strong, assertive, and decisive. It represents individual power, leadership, and self-confidence. This energy drives action, helping one to take charge of situations and express personal authority with clarity.

Feminine Aspect (Receptive, Empowered Intuition): The feminine energy of the solar plexus is about inner strength and personal transformation. It relates to the wisdom that arises from self-awareness and nurturing one's empowerment. The feminine aspect involves emotional intelligence and the ability to find strength through surrender to one's higher self or intuition.

4. Heart Chakra (Anahata) – Love, Compassion, Emotional Balance

Masculine Aspect (Active, Protective Love): The masculine aspect of the heart chakra is about protective love, loyalty, and strengthening relationships. It represents the active giving of love, such as providing for others and being a pillar of emotional support. This energy is linked to action-oriented care, compassion, and loyalty in relationships.

Feminine Aspect (Receptive, Unconditional Love): The feminine energy of the heart chakra embodies unconditional love, compassion, and empathy. It is the ability to receive love and be open to emotional vulnerability while offering selfless love. Feminine heart energy reflects nurturing and empathy, with an expansive, inclusive love that transcends boundaries.

5. Throat Chakra (Vishuddha) – Communication, Self-Expression, Truth

Masculine Aspect (Active, Direct Expression): The masculine energy of the throat chakra is about assertive communication, directness, and clarity of speech. It is the ability to speak one's truth confidently, take the lead in discussions, and project one's voice. This energy is active and often used in leadership, advocacy, or making decisions.

Feminine Aspect (Receptive, Intuitive Expression): The feminine aspect of the throat chakra is more about listening, intuitive expression, and the power of soft speech. It is about the ability to express oneself gently and receive the truths of others with understanding. The feminine energy of the throat is connected to nurturing conversation, emotional expression, and the wisdom of listening.

6. Third Eye Chakra (Ajna) – Intuition, Clarity, Mental Focus

Masculine Aspect (Active, Logical Insight): The masculine energy of the third eye chakra represents clarity, focus, and rational understanding. This energy is connected to mental clarity, the active pursuit of wisdom, and decision-making based on logical insights. It is also tied to strategic thinking and awareness of the big picture.

Feminine Aspect (Receptive, Intuitive Perception): The feminine aspect of the third eye is about heightened intuition, inner wisdom, and psychic sensitivity. It is the ability to perceive beyond the obvious and access the deeper truths of the subconscious. Feminine third-eye energy is about tapping into spiritual knowledge, intuition, and inner vision that comes from surrender and receptivity.

7. Crown Chakra (Sahasrara) – Spiritual Connection, Higher Consciousness

Masculine Aspect (Active, Divine Will): The masculine energy of the crown chakra is about higher consciousness and the active seeking of truth. It relates to the desire to connect with the divine or the universal and to transcend self-limitations in pursuit of higher knowledge. It is the pursuit of enlightenment, spiritual action, and the quest for truth in the larger universe.

Feminine Aspect (Receptive, Divine Wisdom): The feminine energy of the crown chakra is about receiving divine inspiration, spiritual awakening, and surrender to the higher realms of consciousness. It is the receptive, transcendent energy that connects one to the universe and to a higher power. Feminine crown energy is about receiving enlightenment and opening oneself to the flow of divine wisdom, which transcends intellectual understanding.

Integrating the Male and Female Aspects:

The male and female aspects of each chakra represent the dynamic interplay of active and receptive energies, which must be balanced for harmony and well-being. The masculine energy tends to be more assertive, outward, and goal-oriented, while the feminine energy is more nurturing, inward, and intuitive. Both energies are necessary for full chakra activation and balance, and each individual may experience these energies in different ways, depending on their personal makeup, life circumstances, and spiritual journey.

By honoring both masculine and feminine energies in each chakra, we cultivate a deeper sense of wholeness and balance, enabling the free flow of energy and enhancing personal growth, healing, and spiritual evolution.

CHAPTER VIII

CHAKRAS AND ITS WHY OF PURPOSE

Exploring the chakras and their connection to the "why" of purpose involves understanding how each chakra relates to the deeper motivations, desires, and energies that drive us in life. The purpose in the context of chakras is not just about career goals or life missions; it is about aligning with our authentic self, the flow of universal energy, and our spiritual journey. The purpose of each chakra is often reflected in the way it influences various aspects of our physical, emotional, mental, and spiritual existence.

1. Root Chakra (Muladhara) – The Purpose of Stability and Survival

Purpose: The root chakra is fundamentally concerned with our basic survival needs—such as food, shelter, safety, and stability. Its purpose is to ground us in the physical world, helping us feel secure and protected. It forms the foundation for everything else in life, ensuring we have the stability to pursue higher goals.

Why of Purpose: The purpose of the root chakra is to provide the security needed to exist and thrive. It's about feeling rooted in reality and ensuring that we have the basic resources to live and grow in a balanced way. When this chakra is in alignment, it allows us to have a sense of belonging and the right to exist fully in the world.

2. Sacral Chakra (Svadhisthana) – The Purpose of Creativity, Joy, and Relationships

Purpose: The sacral chakra governs emotions, pleasure, and creativity. Its purpose is to help us experience life's pleasures—through creative expression, sexuality, and emotionally fulfilling relationships. It is also connected to our creative potential, encouraging us to be authentic and to experience the joy of being.

Why of Purpose: The purpose of the sacral chakra is to invite us to connect deeply with others and with our own creative energy.

It helps us feel and experience life fully—through emotions, creativity, and the beauty of intimate connection. This chakra's purpose is to help us understand that our emotional and creative fulfillment is an essential part of our human experience and spiritual growth.

3. Solar Plexus Chakra (Manipura) – The Purpose of Personal Power and Self-Confidence

Purpose: The solar plexus chakra is the center of personal power, self-confidence, and willpower. Its purpose is to help us assert ourselves, take charge of our lives, and make decisions that align with our personal values. This chakra is deeply tied to the idea of purpose through its connection to individual identity and the ability to manifest our desires into the physical world.

Why of Purpose: The purpose of the solar plexus chakra is to give us the inner strength and confidence to pursue our life's purpose with clarity and direction. It is the energetic center from which we set intentions and take action to shape our reality, helping us to realize that personal empowerment is essential to fulfilling our higher purpose.

4. Heart Chakra (Anahata) – The Purpose of Love and Compassion

Purpose: The heart chakra is the seat of love, compassion, and empathy. Its purpose is to help us form meaningful connections with others, offering and receiving unconditional love. It is also the bridge between the lower chakras (focused on survival and personal power) and the upper chakras (focused on higher consciousness), helping to integrate self-love with love for others.

Why of Purpose: The purpose of the heart chakra is to help us realize that love and compassion are central to our existence and spiritual journey. It encourages us to cultivate the love that connects us with the divine, others, and ultimately, ourselves. The heart chakra teaches that our highest purpose in life is to love and be loved—transforming both ourselves and the world around us.

5. Throat Chakra (Vishuddha) – The Purpose of Communication and Self-Expression

Purpose: The throat chakra is the center of communication, self-expression, and truth. Its purpose is to help us speak our truth, express ourselves authentically, and communicate effectively with others. This chakra governs our voice, not just in the literal sense, but also in how we express our inner thoughts, creativity, and spiritual insights.

Why of Purpose: The purpose of the throat chakra is to help us find and express our unique voice—to speak our truth with integrity. It is through this chakra that we communicate our authentic self to the world. It also connects us with our spiritual truth and helps us express our soul's purpose through words, art, or other forms of creative expression.

6. Third Eye Chakra (Ajna) – The Purpose of Intuition and Inner Vision

Purpose: The third eye chakra is the center of intuition, wisdom, and spiritual insight. Its purpose is to help us connect with our inner wisdom and the higher consciousness that guides our spiritual journey. It enables us to see beyond the physical realm and access the intuitive knowledge that helps us navigate life's challenges and understand our true purpose.

Why of Purpose: The purpose of the third eye chakra is to provide the inner sight needed to understand the bigger picture of life. It allows us to perceive our spiritual path and recognize the deeper meaning behind our experiences. When activated, it helps us access higher states of consciousness, enabling us to align more closely with our life's purpose and our true essence.

7. Crown Chakra (Sahasrara) – The Purpose of Divine Connection and Enlightenment

Purpose: The crown chakra is the center of spiritual connection, enlightenment, and the divine consciousness. Its purpose is to help us experience a deep sense of connection with the universe, the divine, and the greater collective. This chakra governs our sense of oneness with all of creation and helps us transcend the ego, allowing us to live in alignment with our higher self and the divine plan.

Why of Purpose: The purpose of the crown chakra is to help us experience unity with the divine, realize our spiritual nature, and understand the transcendent meaning of our lives. It provides the wisdom and clarity needed to understand our true purpose as spiritual beings having a human experience. It teaches that our ultimate purpose is to live in alignment with divine will and to express that unity in every aspect of our lives.

When all the chakras are balanced and aligned, they create a holistic understanding of the why behind our existence.

When we balance our chakras, we are better equipped to discover and live out our true purpose, both on a personal and spiritual level, leading to a more meaningful and fulfilling existence.

Summary:

1. The root chakra grounds us in the present moment and provides the stability needed to pursue higher goals.
2. The sacral chakra opens us to creativity and pleasure, reminding us that joy and emotional fulfillment are key aspects of our purpose.
3. The solar plexus chakra empowers us to take action and make choices that align with our individual will.
4. The heart chakra teaches that love is the center of our purpose, both in relation to ourselves and others.
5. The throat chakra encourages us to express our truth, speak up for what we believe in, and communicate our inner wisdom.
6. The third eye chakra helps us understand the deeper meaning of life and trust our intuition in guiding our purpose.
7. The crown chakra connects us to the divine and helps us align with a higher plan, ultimately allowing us to see that our purpose is part of a much larger spiritual journey.

When you have the inner urge to unfold the mystery of why? you have become a seeker of truth.

CHAPTER IX

CHAKRAS AND KARMA

Chakras and karma are deeply interwoven concepts in many spiritual traditions, especially in systems rooted in Indian philosophy.

By understanding how karma shapes your chakra system, you gain the tools to transform both personal and spiritual life.

Karma is the principle of cause and effect. Every action (thought, word, or deed) generates residual energy that influences future outcomes. Each chakra holds karmic imprints from past actions. Karmic imprints is of three types:

1. Sanchita Karma: Accumulated karma from past lives.
2. Prarabdha Karma: Karma currently being experienced in this life.
3. Kriyamana Karma: Karma being created by present actions.

Healing Karma Through Chakras:

Balancing and unblocking chakras can release karmic patterns, aiding spiritual growth.

Balancing and activating chakras, you can release negative karmic cycles and create positive energy flows.

As you transcend lower chakras and activate higher ones (Ajna and Sahasrara), you're said to move beyond karmic entanglements, aligning with higher consciousness.

Ckakra specific techniques:

1. Root Chakra (Muladhara): The Foundation of Karmic Roots

Karma Type: Collective and ancestral karma.

Dynamics: The root chakra carries karmic imprints from familial and ancestral experiences. If past generations experienced trauma like displacement or scarcity, this may manifest as deep-seated fear or insecurity in your life.

Signs of Karmic Imbalance: Financial struggles - Fear of change - Chronic health issues in the legs or lower back

Healing Practices: Grounding exercises (walking barefoot, connecting with nature)

2. Sacral Chakra (Svadhisthana): The Karmic Seat of Emotions

Karma Type: Emotional and relationship karma.

Dynamics: The sacral chakra governs how we express emotions, engage in relationships, and experience pleasure. Karmic patterns here often stem from unresolved attachments, guilt, or misuse of creative energy in past lives.

Signs of Karmic Imbalance: Unhealthy relationships or co-dependency - Suppressed emotions or overindulgence in pleasures - Reproductive or urinary issues

Healing Practices: Creative outlets like art or dance

Water rituals(bathing) to cleanse emotional energy.

3. Solar Plexus Chakra (Manipura): The Karmic Repository of Power

Karma Type: Power dynamics and self-esteem.

Dynamics: This chakra is where karmic lessons about personal power and ego are stored. Patterns of over-dominance or submissiveness in past lives often manifest as control issues or lack of confidence.

Signs of Karmic Imbalance: Digestive issues - Perfectionism or procrastination - Fear of failure or excessive competitiveness

Healing Practices: Sunlight exposure and fire meditations

4. Heart Chakra (Anahata): The Bridge Between Karma and Liberation

Karma Type: Relationship and forgiveness karma.

Dynamics: The heart chakra holds karmic ties to love, compassion, and forgiveness. Pain from betrayal or grief can create karmic knots that block the flow of unconditional love.

Signs of Karmic Imbalance:Inability to forgive or trust - Recurring relationship issues - Respiratory or circulatory problems

Healing Practices: Helping people in need

5. Throat Chakra (Vishuddha): Karmic Truth and Expression

Karma Type: Communication and authenticity karma.

Dynamics: Karma here arises from suppressing truth or misusing speech in past lives.

Signs of Karmic Imbalance: Fear of speaking up - Gossiping or difficulty listening - Throat or thyroid issues

Healing Practices: Journaling or vocal exercises

6. Third Eye Chakra (Ajna): Karmic Vision and Wisdom

Karma Type: Spiritual and intuitive karma.

Dynamics: Past-life misuse of spiritual knowledge or ignoring intuition can block this chakra. It governs your ability to see beyond illusion and understand karmic patterns.

Signs of Karmic Imbalance: Lack of clarity or poor decision-making - Nightmares or headaches - Distrust of intuition

Healing Practices: Visualization techniques - visualise that things are going right for you

7. Crown Chakra (Sahasrara): Karmic Liberation

Karma Type: Divine connection and liberation karma.

Dynamics: The crown chakra represents the dissolution of karmic cycles. A blocked crown chakra suggests resistance to spiritual evolution or attachment to material desires.

Signs of Karmic Imbalance: Disconnection from spirituality - Feeling purposeless or overly attached to ego - Migraines or neurological issues

Healing Practices: Meditation on universal consciousness - simple prayers

Karmic Knots (Granthis) and Chakra Blockages

The granthis are specific knots of karmic energy that block the flow of kundalini energy through the chakras:

Brahma Granthi (Root and Sacral Chakra): Blocks attachment to survival and pleasure.

Vishnu Granthi (Solar Plexus and Heart Chakra): Tied to ego and emotional attachments.

Rudra Granthi (Throat and Third Eye Chakra): Prevents spiritual liberation due to illusions and fear.

Untangling Karmic Knots (Granthis) and Chakra Blockages

Akashic Records: Exploring the Akashic Records with an expert, can reveal the root karmic causes tied to specific chakras.

Past-Life Regression Therapy: Hypnotherapy can uncover and resolve karmic patterns stored in chakras.

Dynamic Energy Clearing: Combining chakra visualization, affirmations, and breathwork to dissolve karmic imprints.

Integrated Chakra Therapy: Engage all chakras simultaneously through sound healing (e.g., Tibetan singing bowls) to balance karma holistically.

CHAPTER X

CHAKRAS AND PHYSIOLOGY

The relationships between each chakra and various physiological functions, including the body's organs, systems, and the flow of energy within the body. Understanding these connections can help support physical health, improve vitality, and promote well-being.

By maintaining balance in the chakras, we support optimal physiological functioning, emotional health, and spiritual growth.

1. Root Chakra (Muladhara) – Survival, Stability, and the Body's Structure

Location: The Root Chakra is located at the base of the spine, near the perineum.

Physiological Associations: The Root Chakra governs the adrenal glands, the bones, and the immune system. It is directly linked to the lower body structure, including the legs, feet, pelvis, and large intestine.

Body Systems: It influences the skeletal system, particularly the bones of the legs and the pelvis. It also plays a role in the body's ability to detoxify and excrete waste through the large intestine.

Key Glands/Organs: The Root Chakra is associated with the adrenal glands (which release adrenaline and cortisol) and the large intestine, affecting digestion and elimination. The adrenal glands also regulate stress responses and metabolism.

Physiological Imbalances: When the Root Chakra is imbalanced or blocked, individuals may experience physical symptoms like lower back pain, sciatica, leg cramps, constipation, or problems with the immune system (frequent colds or infections).

Psychological symptoms of insecurity, fear, and anxiety often accompany these physical ailments.

2. Sacral Chakra (Svadhisthana) – Emotions, Sensuality, and Creativity

Location: The Sacral Chakra is located just below the navel, about two inches below the belly button closer to the reproductive organ in the pelvic region.

Physiological Associations: The Sacral Chakra is linked to the reproductive organs, kidneys, bladder, and the circulatory system. It also governs the pelvic area, the lower abdomen, and the digestive organs.

Body Systems: This chakra influences the reproductive system, including the ovaries, uterus, and testes. It plays a role in the circulation of fluids (like blood and lymph) and impacts kidney function and urinary health.

Key Glands/Organs: The Sacral Chakra is associated with the reproductive organs (ovaries, uterus, testes), kidneys, bladder, and the lower digestive organs, such as the large and small intestines.

Physiological Imbalances: Blockages in the Sacral Chakra may lead to physical symptoms such as lower abdominal pain, urinary tract infections, kidney issues, or menstrual irregularities. Infertility and sexual dysfunction (like impotence, lack of libido, or painful intercourse) can also manifest from an unbalanced Sacral Chakra.

Emotionally, this can manifest as guilt, shame, or repression of feelings.

3. Solar Plexus Chakra (Manipura) – Personal Power, Confidence, and Metabolism

Location: The Solar Plexus Chakra is located above the navel, in the upper abdomen, near the diaphragm.

Physiological Associations: The Solar Plexus Chakra is associated with the pancreas, liver, digestive organs, and the adrenal glands. It plays a role in the body's metabolism, digestion, and energy production.

Body Systems: This chakra governs the digestive system and is directly connected to the stomach, liver, pancreas, gallbladder, and intestines. It influences the body's ability to metabolize food and convert it into energy.

Key Glands/Organs: The Solar Plexus Chakra is linked to the pancreas (which produces insulin and regulates blood sugar), liver, and digestive organs. It also affects the autonomic nervous system, particularly the sympathetic system (fight or flight).

Physiological Imbalances: When the Solar Plexus Chakra is blocked or out of balance, individuals may experience digestive issues such as bloating, indigestion, heartburn, and poor metabolism. Chronic stress can lead to ulcers, blood sugar imbalances, or problems with the liver and gallbladder.

Emotional symptoms such as low self-esteem, lack of motivation, and feelings of powerlessness may also arise.

4. Heart Chakra (Anahata) – Love, Compassion, and Cardiovascular Health

Location: The Heart Chakra is located in the center of the chest, near the heart and lungs.

Physiological Associations: The Heart Chakra is connected to the heart, lungs, thymus gland, and circulatory system. It also affects the immune system.

Body Systems: This chakra governs the cardiovascular system, influencing heart rate, blood circulation, and respiration. It also affects the thymus gland, which is important for immune system regulation.

Key Glands/Organs: The Heart Chakra is directly linked to the heart, lungs, thymus gland, and the circulation of blood throughout the body.

Physiological Imbalances: When the Heart Chakra is blocked or imbalanced, individuals may experience cardiovascular issues such as high blood pressure, heart disease, lung conditions, or respiratory problems. Symptoms may include tightness in the chest, shallow breathing, or irregular heartbeat.

Emotional imbalances associated with the Heart Chakra, like grief, depression, or difficulty expressing love, can contribute to these physical issues.

5. Throat Chakra (Vishuddha) – Communication and Respiratory Health

Location: The Throat Chakra is located at the base of the throat, around the neck and vocal cords.

Physiological Associations: The Throat Chakra is associated with the thyroid gland, the vocal cords, the respiratory system, and the neck and shoulders. It governs the ability to express ourselves verbally and non-verbally.

Body Systems: This chakra governs the respiratory system, particularly the lungs, throat, and mouth, and plays a role in communication, vocalization, and the expression of words. It also influences the thyroid, which regulates metabolism.

Key Glands/Organs: The Throat Chakra is linked to the thyroid gland, vocal cords, throat, lungs, and shoulders.

Physiological Imbalances: When the Throat Chakra is out of balance, individuals may experience throat issues such as sore throat, hoarseness, or thyroid problems (e.g., hypothyroidism or hyperthyroidism). Respiratory issues like asthma, bronchitis, or difficulty breathing may also arise.

Emotionally, a blocked Throat Chakra may lead to difficulty expressing oneself, speaking one's truth, or fear of communication.

6. Third Eye Chakra (Ajna) – Intuition, Vision, and the Nervous System

Location: The Third Eye Chakra is located between the eyebrows, slightly above the bridge of the nose, and is associated with the brain and the pineal gland.

Physiological Associations: The Third Eye Chakra is associated with the brain, the pineal gland, and the nervous system. It governs mental processes, intuition, and perception, as well as the overall functioning of the nervous system.

Body Systems: This chakra influences the brain, central nervous system, and eye function. It plays a role in regulating the body's mental processes and cognitive abilities, including memory, intuition, and clarity of thought.

Key Glands/Organs: The Third Eye Chakra is linked to the pineal gland (which regulates sleep-wake cycles and melatonin production) and the brain, influencing cognitive functions, mental clarity, and intuition.

Physiological Imbalances: Blockages in the Third Eye Chakra may lead to headaches, vision problems, and disorders of the nervous system. Problems with memory, mental clarity, or concentration may also arise.

Emotionally, it can manifest as confusion, inability to trust intuition, or mental fog.

7. Crown Chakra (Sahasrara) – Spiritual Connection and the Central Nervous System

Location: The Crown Chakra is located at the top of the head, at the crown of the skull.

Physiological Associations: The Crown Chakra is associated with the central nervous system, the brain, and the pineal gland. It governs the body's connection to spiritual consciousness, higher states of awareness, and the unification of body and spirit.

Body Systems: This chakra influences the brain's higher functions and overall nervous system health. It also affects the body's ability to connect to higher spiritual realms and access divine or universal wisdom.

Key Glands/Organs: The Crown Chakra is linked to the pineal gland and the brain, particularly the cerebral cortex and the limbic system, which govern higher brain functions and spiritual experiences.

Physiological Imbalances: When the Crown Chakra is blocked or imbalanced, individuals may experience neurological problems such as migraines, poor memory, or mental confusion.

A lack of spiritual connection or a sense of disconnection from the world around them can also be associated with this imbalance.

CHAPTER XI

CHAKRAS AND PHYSICAL HEALING

Chakras and physical healing are intricately connected, because the chakra system is believed to influence not only our emotional, mental, and spiritual well-being but also our physical health. The idea is that each chakra is linked to specific organs, tissues, and body systems, and imbalances in these energy centers can manifest as physical ailments. Through chakra healing, it's possible to restore balance to the body's energy flow, which can, in turn, promote physical health and healing.

By understanding the relationship between the chakras and physical health, we can use chakra work to support healing at both an energetic and physical level. This holistic approach encourages overall well-being and vitality.

How Chakras Influence Physical Health

Chakras are energy centers that govern various aspects of life, including the body's health. When there is a blockage, imbalance, or underactive energy in a particular chakra, it can lead to physical symptoms or conditions related to the body part that chakra governs. Healing and balancing the chakras through conscious energy work, mindfulness, and physical practices like yoga can restore vitality and promote physical healing.

Chakras and Their Role in Physical Healing

1. Chakra (Muladhara): Physical Body, Spine, Legs, and Feet

Physical Areas Affected:

The root chakra governs the skeletal system, particularly the spine, hips, legs, feet, and bones. It also influences the adrenals and large intestine.

Blockages or imbalances can manifest as lower back pain, sciatica, leg or foot problems, fatigue, or issues with elimination (constipation, diarrhea).

Physical Healing Techniques:

Grounding Exercises: Walking barefoot, standing with feet firmly planted on the ground, or visualizing roots connecting to the earth helps to balance this chakra.

Yoga Poses: Poses like Mountain Pose, Warrior I, and Tree Pose activate and stabilize the root chakra, promoting better posture and physical strength.

Breathwork: Deep, diaphragmatic breathing can help release tension in the lower body and improve blood circulation.

Affirmation: "I am grounded and safe in my body."

2. Sacral Chakra (Svadhisthana): Reproductive Organs, Kidneys, Lower Abdomen

Physical Areas Affected:

The sacral chakra governs the reproductive organs (ovaries, testicles), kidneys, bladder, lower abdomen, and digestion.

Imbalances here can lead to issues such as lower back pain, menstrual irregularities, urinary problems, kidney infections, pelvic problems, and digestive disorders like IBS(irritable bowel syndrome) or bloating.

Physical Healing Techniques:

Pelvic Exercises: Gentle pelvic rocking, hip-opening yoga poses (e.g., Butterfly Pose, Pigeon Pose), and other movements that engage the pelvic area help to stimulate and balance this chakra.

Hydration: Drinking plenty of water supports this chakra, as it governs fluidity and the water element.

Creative Expression: Engaging in creative activities like painting, dancing, or writing can release emotional blockages tied to the sacral chakra.

Affirmation: "I embrace my body's ability to heal."

3. Solar Plexus Chakra (Manipura): Digestive System, Liver, Gallbladder

Physical Areas Affected:

The solar plexus chakra governs the digestive system, including the stomach, liver, gallbladder, pancreas, and small intestine.

Physical symptoms of imbalance might include digestive issues (acid reflux, indigestion, bloating), liver problems, and metabolic disorders like diabetes or hypoglycemia.

Physical Healing Techniques:

Digestive Support: Practices like mindful eating, slow chewing, and incorporating warming foods (ginger, and turmeric) can help to support digestion.

Core Strengthening: Yoga poses that engage the core (e.g., Boat Pose, Plank Pose, and Warrior III) help activate the solar plexus chakra.

Breathwork: Abdominal breathing (diaphragmatic breathing) is excellent for stimulating digestion and clearing blockages in the solar plexus.

Affirmation: "I nourish my body with healthy food."

4. Heart Chakra (Anahata): Heart, Lungs, Circulatory System

Physical Areas Affected:

The heart chakra governs the heart, lungs, chest, arms, and hands. It is also linked to the circulatory system.

Physical ailments related to this chakra might include heart disease, respiratory issues, high blood pressure, asthma, upper back and shoulder pain, and immune system imbalances.

Physical Healing Techniques:

Heart-Opening Yoga: Poses such as Camel Pose, Cobra Pose, and Bridge Pose stretch and open the chest, promoting heart and lung health.

Deep Breathing: Practices like deep abdominal breathing or pranayama (breath control) can improve lung function and circulation.

Emotional Healing: Engage in practices that cultivate love, forgiveness, and compassion, as emotional blockages often manifest physically in the heart and lungs.

Affirmation: "I am love, and my heart is healthy and compassionate."

5. Throat Chakra (Vishuddha): Throat, Neck, Ears, Mouth, Teeth

Physical Areas Affected:

The throat chakra governs the throat, neck, jaw, mouth, ears, and thyroid.

Blockages or imbalances in this chakra can lead to conditions such as sore throats, thyroid imbalances, jaw tension, neck pain, laryngitis, or ear infections.

Physical Healing Techniques:

Vocal Expression: Regularly speaking, singing, or chanting can help clear blockages in the throat chakra.

Neck and Shoulder Stretches: Gentle stretches for the neck and shoulders, such as neck rolls and ear-to-shoulder stretches, can relieve tension.

Hydration and Healthy Diet: Staying hydrated and consuming foods that support thyroid function (like iodine-rich foods) can help maintain balance in this chakra.

Affirmation: "I express confidently, and my throat is healthy."

6. Third Eye Chakra (Ajna): Eyes, Brain, Nervous System

Physical Areas Affected:

The third eye chakra governs the eyes, brain, nervous system, and pituitary gland.

Imbalances can manifest as vision problems, headaches, migraines, neurological issues, or cognitive challenges such as memory problems or brain fog.

Physical Healing Techniques:

Eye Exercises: Gentle eye movements and focusing on objects at varying distances can help improve eye health.

Meditation and Visualization: Practices such as focusing on the space between the eyebrows (the location of the third eye) can stimulate mental clarity and improve concentration.

Cognitive Stimulation: Engage in mental exercises like puzzles, reading, or learning new skills to boost brain function.

Affirmation: "I trust my inner wisdom."

7. Crown Chakra (Sahasrara): Brain, Nervous System, Skin

Physical Areas Affected:

The crown chakra governs the brain, nervous system, and skin.

Physical symptoms of imbalance may include neurological issues, headaches, sensitivity to light or sound, or skin problems like rashes or dryness.

Physical Healing Techniques:

Meditation and Silence: Practices that promote mental stillness and spiritual connection, such as deep meditation or quiet contemplation, help activate the crown chakra.

Cleansing and Detoxing: Detoxifying the body through clean eating, fasting, or gentle cleansing can help promote balance in the crown chakra.

Light Therapy: Exposure to natural light or visualizing violet or white light during meditation can help open and balance the crown chakra.

Affirmation: "I am divine wisdom."

Shortcut for Physical Healing: Walking , Simple physical activities.

CHAPTER XII

CHAKRAS AND PSYCHOLOGY

The chakras, as centers of energy and consciousness within the body, not only influence our physical well-being but also play a profound role in shaping our psychological states, behaviors, and emotional experiences.

The chakra system provides a framework for understanding the interplay between body, mind, and spirit, offering insights into how our psychological health can be supported by balancing and harmonizing these energy centers.

1. Root Chakra (Muladhara) – Psychological Foundation and Security

Location: The Root Chakra is located at the base of the spine, near the perineum.

Psychological Functions: The Root Chakra is the foundation of our psychological stability. It represents our basic needs for survival, safety, and security. When this chakra is balanced, we feel grounded, stable, and confident in our ability to face life's challenges.

Emotional Themes: Fear, anxiety, and insecurity are the primary emotional imbalances that arise when the Root Chakra is out of alignment. Psychologically, this chakra is connected to our sense of self-worth and our ability to trust in ourselves and the world around us.

Developmental Stage: The Root Chakra corresponds to the earliest stages of human development, where basic needs for food, shelter, and emotional safety are established. Psychologically, this stage of life (infancy and early childhood) is when we learn to trust or mistrust our environment and caregivers.

Imbalances: When the Root Chakra is blocked or imbalanced, individuals may experience fear, chronic anxiety, or feelings of instability. Issues like financial insecurity, relationship problems, or a lack of grounding can stem from an imbalanced Root Chakra.

2. Sacral Chakra (Svadhisthana) – Emotions, Creativity, and Sexuality

Location: The Sacral Chakra is located just below the navel, about two inches below the belly button and closer to the reproductive organs, in the pelvic region.

Psychological Functions: The Sacral Chakra is the center of emotions, creativity, and sexual identity. It governs how we relate to our feelings, creativity, sensuality, and intimacy. A balanced Sacral Chakra fosters emotional fluidity and healthy relationships with our feelings and desires.

Emotional Themes: Guilt, shame, and emotional repression are key psychological patterns that arise when this chakra is out of balance. The Sacral Chakra is strongly connected to our ability to experience pleasure, creativity, and emotional expression.

Developmental Stage: Psychologically, the Sacral Chakra relates to childhood and adolescence, especially during the formative years of emotional development. This stage involves learning how to express emotions, develop healthy sexual relationships, and create meaningful emotional bonds with others.

Imbalances: A blocked or unbalanced Sacral Chakra may lead to emotional instability, unhealthy emotional attachments, or difficulties with intimacy and sexuality. Individuals may struggle with guilt, shame, or fear related to their creative abilities or sexual identity.

3. Solar Plexus Chakra (Manipura) – Personal Power, Confidence, and Self-Esteem

Location: The Solar Plexus Chakra is located above the navel, in the upper abdomen, near the diaphragm.

Psychological Functions: The Solar Plexus Chakra governs personal power, confidence, self-esteem, and our ability to take action. It represents our sense of self and our ability to assert our will in the world. Psychologically, this chakra is connected to our sense of identity and autonomy.

Emotional Themes: When the Solar Plexus Chakra is imbalanced, feelings of inadequacy, low self-esteem, and lack of control can arise. This chakra helps us establish boundaries, assert our needs, and express personal power.

Developmental Stage: This chakra is linked to the psychological stage of early childhood, where we develop our sense of identity and autonomy. This is the stage where we learn to navigate power dynamics and take responsibility for our actions.

Imbalances: If the Solar Plexus Chakra is blocked, individuals may struggle with a lack of confidence, fear of failure, and self-doubt. They may feel powerless, unable to make decisions, or have difficulty setting boundaries with others.

4. Heart Chakra (Anahata) – Love, Compassion, and Emotional Balance

Location: The Heart Chakra is located in the center of the chest, near the heart and lungs.

Psychological Functions: The Heart Chakra is the center of love, compassion, empathy, and emotional balance. It governs how we relate to others in terms of care, affection, and unconditional love. Psychologically, it is deeply connected to our ability to form healthy relationships and give and receive love.

Emotional Themes: When the Heart Chakra is imbalanced, we may experience feelings of emotional isolation, grief, resentment, or emotional coldness. The Heart Chakra is also connected to our ability to forgive and heal emotional wounds.

Developmental Stage: The Heart Chakra corresponds to the period of emotional maturation during adolescence and early adulthood, where we establish deeper connections with others. This stage involves learning how to give and receive love, build trust, and experience emotional intimacy.

Imbalances: An imbalanced Heart Chakra may manifest as a lack of emotional connection, difficulty expressing love, or an inability to forgive. Individuals may also experience chronic grief, fear of abandonment, or difficulty trusting others.

5. Throat Chakra (Vishuddha) – Communication, Expression, and Authenticity

Location: The Throat Chakra is located at the base of the throat, around the neck and vocal cords.

Psychological Functions: The Throat Chakra governs communication, self-expression, and authenticity. It is the center of verbal and non-verbal expression, creativity, and speaking one's truth. Psychologically, this chakra is closely linked to our ability to express ourselves clearly, both in speech and action.

Emotional Themes: When the Throat Chakra is blocked or imbalanced, we may struggle with communication, feeling misunderstood, or unable to express our true thoughts and feelings. This chakra is also associated with our ability to listen actively and engage in meaningful dialogue.

Developmental Stage: The Throat Chakra corresponds to the later stages of childhood and adolescence, when verbal communication and self-expression are developed. This is the period when we learn to speak our truth and express our individuality.

Imbalances: An imbalanced Throat Chakra may result in fear of speaking up, a tendency to suppress one's thoughts or emotions, or feelings of being unheard. Individuals may experience social anxiety, chronic throat issues, or difficulty articulating their needs.

6. Third Eye Chakra (Ajna) – Intuition, Insight, and Mental Clarity

Location: The Third Eye Chakra is located between the eyebrows, slightly above the bridge of the nose, and is associated with the brain and the pineal gland.

Psychological Functions: The Third Eye Chakra is the center of intuition, insight, and mental clarity. It governs our ability to perceive deeper truths, access our inner wisdom, and make sense of abstract concepts. Psychologically, it relates to our cognitive functions, critical thinking, and the ability to see beyond surface appearances.

Emotional Themes: When the Third Eye Chakra is imbalanced, we may struggle with confusion, lack of direction, or an inability to trust our intuition. This chakra is also related to our inner vision, allowing us to understand ourselves and the world around us with greater clarity.

Developmental Stage: The Third Eye Chakra is connected to the maturation of the mind and intellect, especially during adolescence and adulthood. This is the stage where we develop abstract thinking, perception, and problem-solving skills.

Imbalances: A blocked Third Eye Chakra can lead to mental fog, confusion, and a lack of direction in life. Individuals may struggle with decision-making, feel disconnected from their inner wisdom, or have difficulty focusing and concentrating.

7. Crown Chakra (Sahasrara) – Spirituality, Consciousness, and Transcendence

Location: The Crown Chakra is located at the top of the head, at the crown of the skull.

Psychological Functions: The Crown Chakra represents our connection to the higher self, spirituality, and universal consciousness. Psychologically, it governs our sense of purpose, the quest for meaning, and our connection to something greater than ourselves.

Emotional Themes: When the Crown Chakra is imbalanced, we may feel disconnected, spiritually lost, or lacking in purpose. This chakra is associated with the search for transcendence and the awareness of our place in the universe.

Developmental Stage: The Crown Chakra is linked to the spiritual awakening process, often occurring later in life, when individuals seek to understand their deeper purpose and connection to the divine. This stage is characterized by a longing for spiritual fulfillment and the realization of inner peace.

Imbalances: If the Crown Chakra is blocked, individuals may experience feelings of spiritual emptiness, existential crisis, or a sense of isolation. They may struggle to find meaning in life or feel disconnected from their higher self.

Chakra Imbalances and Psychological Disorders

An imbalance in any of the chakras can manifest as psychological issues, and in many cases, chakra imbalances are intertwined with mental health conditions.

Root Chakra Imbalance: May contribute to anxiety disorders, panic attacks, and phobias related to safety and survival.

Sacral Chakra Imbalance: Can lead to emotional instability, depression, and issues with intimacy or sexual dysfunction.

Solar Plexus Chakra Imbalance: May manifest as low self-esteem, chronic stress, eating disorders, and issues with authority or power struggles.

Heart Chakra Imbalance: Can contribute to depression, emotional coldness, fear of intimacy, and problems with forgiveness.

Throat Chakra Imbalance: May result in social anxiety, communication issues, and difficulties with self-expression.

Third Eye Chakra Imbalance: Can lead to confusion, lack of clarity, decision-making difficulties, and problems trusting one's intuition.

Crown Chakra Imbalance: Can cause spiritual disconnection, existential anxiety, and a lack of purpose or direction in life.

CHAPTER XIII

CHAKRAS AND MENTAL HEALING

Chakras play a crucial role in mental health and healing, as they are not only centers of energy but also areas where emotional and mental imbalances can manifest. Each chakra is associated with specific mental and emotional functions, and blockages or imbalances in these areas can lead to mental health challenges such as stress, anxiety, depression, confusion, and more.

Each chakra is linked to a specific mental and emotional states. When these centers are in balance, we experience mental clarity, emotional stability, and a sense of inner peace.

1. Root Chakra (Muladhara): Security, Stability, Grounding

Mental Health Influence:

The root chakra is foundational, and when it is unbalanced, it can lead to feelings of insecurity, fear, anxiety, and a lack of grounding. You might feel disconnected from your body, overwhelmed, or uncertain about your place in the world.

Common mental health challenges include chronic stress, fear-based thinking, and a sense of instability.

Mental Healing Techniques:

Grounding Practices: Engage in activities that help you feel more grounded, like walking in nature, sitting on the earth, or doing mindful breathing.

Mindfulness Meditation: Focus on the present moment and bring your awareness back to the body to feel more anchored.

Affirmation: "I trust in the process of life."

2. Sacral Chakra (Svadhisthana): Creativity, Emotional Expression, Relationships

Mental Health Influence:

The sacral chakra governs emotions, creativity, and relationships. When it's out of balance, you may experience emotional instability, difficulty in expressing yourself creatively, or challenges in your relationships.

Common issues include depression, emotional repression, guilt, shame, and a fear of intimacy.

Mental Healing Techniques:

Creative Expression: Engage in activities like painting, writing, or dancing to release emotional blockages and foster self-expression.

Emotional Awareness: Practice journaling or mindfulness to become aware of and release suppressed emotions.

Affirmation: " I am worthy of love and joy."

3. Solar Plexus Chakra (Manipura): Confidence, Willpower, Self-Esteem

Mental Health Influence:

The solar plexus chakra is closely tied to personal power, self-confidence, and the ability to assert oneself. An imbalance here can manifest as low self-esteem, self-doubt, and a lack of motivation.

Mental health issues might include anxiety, fear of failure, or struggles with decision-making and personal boundaries.

Mental Healing Techniques:

Self-Awareness: Engage in practices that help you build self-trust, such as reflecting on your strengths or setting achievable goals.

Empowerment Practices: Practice standing up for yourself, making decisions with confidence, and setting healthy boundaries.

Affirmation: "I am powerful in achieving my goals."

4. Heart Chakra (Anahata): Love, Compassion, Emotional Healing

Mental Health Influence:

The heart chakra governs love, compassion, and emotional healing. When blocked, it can lead to feelings of loneliness, inability to give or receive love, and emotional wounds such as grief, loss, or betrayal.

Common mental health issues include depression, anger, emotional isolation, and difficulty in forgiveness.

Mental Healing Techniques:

Self-Love Practices: Engage in self-care and self-compassion activities. Focus on forgiving yourself and others.

Heart-Centered Meditation: Meditate with a focus on your heart center, cultivating feelings of love, compassion, and forgiveness.

Affirmation: "I am open to giving and receiving love."

5. Throat Chakra (Vishuddha): Communication, Truth, Expression

Mental Health Influence:

The throat chakra is linked to communication, self-expression, and speaking one's truth. When blocked, it can lead to problems with self-expression, fear of speaking up, and an inability to communicate your needs or emotions.

Mental health issues can include anxiety, a feeling of being misunderstood, or social isolation.

Mental Healing Techniques:

Conscious Communication: Practice speaking your truth in a mindful, clear, and authentic way.

Expressive Writing: Journaling or writing about your thoughts and feelings helps release blockages in the throat chakra.

Affirmation: "I speak the truth with confidence."

6. Third Eye Chakra (Ajna): Intuition, Clarity, Insight

Mental Health Influence:

The third eye chakra governs intuition, clarity of thought, and inner wisdom. When imbalanced, it can lead to confusion, lack of direction, poor decision-making, or a disconnection from your inner guidance.

Mental health issues might include brain fog, indecisiveness, anxiety related to uncertainty, or feeling disconnected from a higher purpose.

Mental Healing Techniques:

Meditation for Clarity: Practice mindfulness meditation focused on the third eye, visualizing a sense of inner knowing and clear sight.

Visualization: Engage in visualization practices where you picture yourself clearly seeing the right path forward.

Affirmation: "I trust my intuition."

7. Crown Chakra (Sahasrara): Spiritual Connection, Purpose, Enlightenment

Mental Health Influence:

The crown chakra is associated with spiritual connection, enlightenment, and a sense of purpose. When out of balance, it can cause feelings of spiritual disconnection, lack of purpose, and mental burnout.

Mental health issues include existential crises, feelings of hopelessness, a lack of direction, and difficulty connecting with the larger universe.

Mental Healing Techniques:

Spiritual Practices: Engage in spiritual practices that foster a sense of connection to something greater, such as prayer, meditation, or contemplation.

Mindfulness: Practicing stillness and embracing the present moment helps connect with the crown chakra's energy.

Affirmation: "I trust the universe's plan for me."

Shortcut for Mental Healing: Reading, Learning, Writing, Creating

CHAPTER XIV

CHAKRAS AND MENTAL CHATTER

Mental chatter, often referred to as the "monkey mind," is the constant stream of thoughts, worries, distractions, and self-talk that can overwhelm us, making it difficult to focus, relax, or connect with our inner selves. This constant mental noise can prevent us from being present, making decisions, or accessing deeper levels of awareness and intuition. The chakras, as centers of energy and consciousness, are deeply connected to the mind and can play a significant role in either amplifying or calming mental chatter.

Each chakra has a unique influence on the quality of our thoughts and mental patterns. When the chakras are imbalanced or blocked, mental chatter can become more chaotic and disruptive, while a balanced and aligned chakra system can help quiet the mind, create clarity, and foster a sense of inner peace.

1. Root Chakra (Muladhara): Quieting Anxiety and Fear-Based Thoughts

Role in Mental Chatter: The root chakra governs our sense of security, stability, and basic survival instincts. When this chakra is imbalanced, we can experience increased anxiety, fear, or feelings of instability. These emotions fuel mental chatter, causing us to overthink and worry about our safety, finances, or place in the world.

Impact on Mental Chatter: Fear and insecurity often lead to a constant flow of anxious thoughts. If we feel unsafe or ungrounded, the mind tends to amplify worries about potential dangers or survival concerns.

How to Calm Mental Chatter through the Root Chakra: Grounding exercises are essential for calming the root chakra. Practices like walking barefoot on the earth, sitting in nature, or visualizing roots extending from your body into the Earth can help anchor the mind, reducing anxiety and quieting the internal noise.

Affirmations for Root Chakra: "I am safe and secure in the present moment."

2. Sacral Chakra (Svadhisthana): Managing Emotional Turmoil and Impulsive Thoughts

Role in Mental Chatter: The sacral chakra is the center of emotions, desires, and creativity. When this chakra is imbalanced, emotional turbulence, guilt, or a lack of self-expression can lead to overwhelming mental chatter. We may overanalyze our emotions, feel conflicted about desires, or experience emotional reactivity that causes the mind to race.

Impact on Mental Chatter: Unresolved emotions or emotional dependency can create repetitive, cyclical thinking, where the mind is stuck in a loop of emotional turmoil, self-doubt, or conflicting desires.

How to Calm Mental Chatter through the Sacral Chakra: To quiet the mind, it's important to process and release emotional blockages. Practices such as journaling, emotional release techniques, or creative self-expression can help clear the emotional fog that fuels mental chatter.

Affirmations for Sacral Chakra: "I honor and express and embrace emotional clarity."

3. Solar Plexus Chakra (Manipura): Overcoming Self-Doubt and Overthinking

Role in Mental Chatter: The solar plexus chakra governs personal power, self-confidence, and will. When this chakra is imbalanced, feelings of inadequacy or lack of control can lead to constant overthinking and mental self-criticism. We may get stuck in a loop of doubt, second-guessing ourselves, and replaying past decisions or mistakes in our minds.

Impact on Mental Chatter: A lack of confidence and a tendency to worry about external opinions or outcomes can fuel excessive mental chatter, often leading to mental exhaustion and indecisiveness.

How to Calm Mental Chatter through the Solar Plexus Chakra: Strengthening self-confidence and willpower is key to reducing mental chatter in the solar plexus. Engage in practices that boost self-esteem and assertiveness, such as goal-setting, affirmations, or small acts of bravery.

Affirmations for Solar Plexus Chakra: "I embrace my personal power."

4. Heart Chakra (Anahata): Quieting Emotional Overload

Role in Mental Chatter: The heart chakra governs love, compassion, and emotional balance. When this chakra is imbalanced, we may become overwhelmed with emotional thoughts—whether they are related to relationships, past trauma, or self-love. This emotional overload can fuel mental chatter, causing us to overthink interactions, past wounds, or feelings of rejection.

Impact on Mental Chatter: Unhealed emotional wounds, unexpressed love, or a lack of self-compassion can keep the mind in a constant loop of emotional processing, preventing mental stillness and peace.

How to Calm Mental Chatter through the Heart Chakra: Healing emotional wounds and opening the heart chakra allows for deeper peace. Practices like forgiveness, self-love rituals, or focusing on compassion can help quiet the emotional chatter that clouds mental clarity.

Affirmations for Heart Chakra: "I allow peace to fill my heart."

5. Throat Chakra (Vishuddha): Releasing the Need for Validation and Control

Role in Mental Chatter: The throat chakra governs communication and self-expression. When imbalanced, we may have an overwhelming desire to control conversations or gain validation through words. This can lead to excessive talking, self-doubt, or an inner dialogue where we are constantly questioning how we are perceived.

Impact on Mental Chatter: A blocked or overactive throat chakra can lead to mental chatter related to self-expression. This could involve worrying about saying the right thing, being afraid to speak the truth, or mentally replaying conversations to see if we were understood or approved of.

How to Calm Mental Chatter through the Throat Chakra: Clearing the throat chakra can involve finding ways to express yourself freely, whether through speaking, writing, or creative expression. Practicing mindful communication and releasing the need for external validation can help reduce mental noise.

Affirmations for Throat Chakra: "I speak the truth with confidence."

6. Third Eye Chakra (Ajna): Quieting Mental Overload and Strengthening Intuition

Role in Mental Chatter: The third eye chakra governs intuition, clarity, and perception. When this chakra is imbalanced, we may experience mental overload or confusion, where our thoughts become scattered and unclear. This can result in an overactive mind that is constantly analyzing, doubting, or second-guessing.

Impact on Mental Chatter: The inability to trust our intuition or the inability to discern between intuition and mental noise can create a constant mental buzz. A cluttered third eye chakra leads to a mind that is full of distractions and confusion.

How to Calm Mental Chatter through the Third Eye Chakra: Strengthening the third eye chakra involves practices that help sharpen intuition and mental clarity, such as meditation, mindfulness, or visualization exercises. Quieting the mind through focused attention can help reduce mental chatter and allow intuitive insights to flow.

Affirmations for Third Eye Chakra: "I trust my inner vision."

7. Crown Chakra (Sahasrara): Quieting the Ego and Transcending Thought Patterns

Role in Mental Chatter: The crown chakra connects us to higher consciousness, spiritual awareness, and oneness with the universe. When the crown chakra is imbalanced, we may experience an overactive mind, filled with repetitive thoughts, distractions, or spiritual confusion. The ego can dominate, creating mental chatter that keeps us focused on the self, rather than the greater universal truth.

Impact on Mental Chatter: The ego's need for control and validation can create persistent mental noise, keeping us disconnected from higher states of consciousness and preventing the quietude necessary for spiritual awakening.

How to Calm Mental Chatter through the Crown Chakra: Practices that connect us to the divine or the collective consciousness, such as meditation, prayer, or surrendering to a higher power, can help quiet the mental chatter that arises from ego-based thinking.

Affirmations for Crown Chakra: "I am connected to the universe."

Summary: Reducing Mental Chatter Through Chakra Balance

Mental chatter can arise from imbalances in any of the chakras. By understanding the specific influence each chakra has on our thoughts and emotional patterns, we can begin to quiet the mind and restore inner peace. Practices such as grounding, emotional release, meditation, and self-expression can help to clear mental clutter, reduce overthinking, and enhance clarity.

When the chakras are balanced, we can cultivate a quieter, more focused mind that allows us to be present, intuitive, and connected to our higher self.

Regular chakra work, including mindfulness and energy healing practices, can help dissolve mental chatter and bring us into a state of mental calm and clarity.

CHAPTER XV

CHAKRAS AND EMOTIONAL HEALING

Chakras and emotional healing are deeply connected, as the chakra system governs not only our physical and mental states but also our emotional well-being. Each chakra is associated with specific emotions, and when these centers are imbalanced or blocked, they can manifest as emotional distress or difficulty in processing emotions.

Each chakra corresponds to a different aspect of our emotional landscape. By understanding the relationship between chakras and emotional states, we can better manage our emotions

1. Root Chakra (Muladhara): Safety, Stability, Survival

Emotional Impact: The root chakra governs our sense of security, survival, and connection to the earth. When imbalanced, it can manifest as feelings of fear, insecurity, anxiety, and emotional instability. You may feel ungrounded or disconnected from others, or even have an overwhelming sense of vulnerability.

Emotional wounds related to this chakra often stem from past traumas, abandonment, or financial instability.

Grounding Practices: Walking barefoot on natural surfaces, spending time in nature, or visualizing roots extending from your body to the earth can help restore a sense of safety and stability.

Affirmations: "I am safe, secure, and grounded."

Breathwork: Deep, steady breathing helps calm the nervous system and promotes a sense of safety.

2. Sacral Chakra (Svadhisthana): Emotions, Creativity, Relationships

Emotional Impact: The sacral chakra governs our emotional expression, creativity, and relationships. When blocked, it can lead to emotional repression, guilt, shame, or an inability to express emotions freely. You may feel disconnected from your own feelings or struggle to form meaningful connections with others.

Unresolved emotions related to past relationships, intimacy, or creativity can cause emotional stagnation.

Creative Expression: Engaging in creative activities such as painting, dancing, or writing can help release emotional tension and allow for the healthy expression of feelings.

Emotional Release: Journaling or engaging in conversations about repressed emotions can help bring suppressed feelings to the surface, allowing for healing.

Affirmations: "I freely express my creativity."

Pelvic Area Movements: Gentle hip movements or yoga poses (like Pigeon Pose) can help release trapped emotions in the sacral region.

3. Solar Plexus Chakra (Manipura): Confidence, Self-Esteem, Personal Power

Emotional Impact: The solar plexus chakra governs our self-esteem, confidence, and personal power. When this chakra is imbalanced, it can lead to feelings of low self-worth, self-doubt, and a lack of motivation or willpower. Emotional wounds related to criticism, rejection, or failure often manifest in the solar plexus chakra, leading to anxiety, anger, or emotional frustration.

Self-Empowerment: Practicing self-affirmations and setting boundaries can help rebuild confidence and a sense of personal power.

Core Strengthening Exercises: Engaging in yoga poses that activate the core, such as Boat Pose or Warrior II, can help you feel more grounded in your personal strength.

Affirmations: "I am worthy of success."

Visualization: Picture yourself achieving your goals and experiencing personal empowerment.

4. Heart Chakra (Anahata): Love, Compassion, Healing Emotional Pain

Emotional Impact: The heart chakra is the center of love, compassion, and emotional healing. When blocked, it can lead to emotional pain, grief, bitterness, and difficulty in giving or receiving love. You may experience feelings of emotional numbness, loneliness, or difficulty in forgiving others (or yourself).

Wounds associated with loss, betrayal, or unmet emotional needs often reside here, causing feelings of sadness and emotional isolation.

Self-Love Practices: Focus on cultivating self-compassion and acceptance. Spend time nurturing yourself and forgiving yourself for past emotional mistakes.

Heart-Opening Yoga: Poses like Camel Pose, Bridge Pose, or Cobra Pose help open the chest and release pent-up emotional energy.

Affirmations: "I forgive myself and all."

Forgiveness Practices: Engage in practices of forgiveness, both towards yourself and others, to release emotional baggage.

5. Throat Chakra (Vishuddha): Communication, Expression of Truth

Emotional Impact: The throat chakra governs communication, self-expression, and speaking your truth. When blocked, it can lead to feelings of frustration, isolation, and anxiety about expressing yourself. You might suppress your emotions or feel misunderstood by others.

Emotional wounds related to feeling unheard, silenced, or not being able to express your truth can create tension and anxiety in this chakra.

Vocal Expression: Practice singing, chanting, or speaking your feelings aloud to release pent-up emotions.

Journaling or Writing: Expressing your emotions through writing can also help clear emotional blockages in the throat area.

Affirmations: "I speak the truth with confidence and clarity."

Neck Stretches: Gentle stretches for the neck and shoulders can help release tension in the throat chakra.

6. Third Eye Chakra (Ajna): Intuition, Mental Clarity, Emotional Awareness

Emotional Impact: The third eye chakra is related to intuition, mental clarity, and insight into your emotions. When blocked, you may struggle with clarity, making it hard to process or understand your emotional state. You might experience confusion, lack of direction, or difficulty in trusting your own inner wisdom.

Emotional challenges in this chakra arise when you have trouble trusting your own feelings or when your intuition is clouded by fear or overthinking.

Meditation for Clarity: Practice focusing on your third eye during meditation, visualizing a deep sense of knowing and emotional clarity.

Mindful Awareness: Engage in mindfulness practices to increase awareness of your thoughts and emotions, helping you understand them with greater clarity.

Affirmations: "I am balanced in my emotions."

Visualization: Visualize yourself seeing your emotions clearly and being able to respond with wisdom.

7. Crown Chakra (Sahasrara): Spiritual Connection, Transcendence of Emotional Pain

Emotional Impact: The crown chakra is the center of spiritual connection, transcendence, and a sense of purpose. When imbalanced, it can lead to feelings of disconnection, isolation, and a lack of meaning or purpose in life.

Emotional challenges related to this chakra often involve feelings of hopelessness, existential despair, or a lack of spiritual fulfillment.

Spiritual Practices: Engage in prayer, meditation, or mindfulness practices to reconnect with a higher power or sense of purpose.

Acceptance and Surrender: Let go of control over life's challenges and trust in the divine flow of life.

Affirmations: "I am connected to the universe."

Shortcut for Emotional Healing: Learn to PAUSE before you react.

CHAPTER XVI

CHAKRAS AND SEXUAL HEALING

Sexuality is sacred. Chakras and sexual healing are deeply connected, as our energy centers govern both our physical, emotional, and spiritual experiences of intimacy and sexuality. Sexuality is not just a physical act but a holistic experience that involves emotional and energetic exchanges, and the state of our chakras can either enhance or block the flow of sexual energy. By understanding how each chakra influences our sexual energy, we can engage in healing practices to improve our sexual health, intimacy, and overall sense of vitality.

Chakra healing offers a powerful way to enhance and heal your sexual energy. By understanding how each chakra influences your sexuality and intimacy, you can use healing techniques to release blockages, restore balance.

1. Root Chakra (Muladhara): Sexual Grounding and Safety

Role of the Root Chakra in Sexual Healing: The root chakra is the foundation of your entire energy system, governing your sense of safety, security, and grounding. It governs your basic survival instincts, including physical well-being, and directly impacts how safe you feel in your body and your environment.

For sexual healing, a balanced root chakra is essential for feeling grounded and secure enough to experience intimacy. When the root chakra is blocked or unbalanced, feelings of fear, insecurity, and anxiety can arise, making it difficult to fully engage in sexual experiences or to feel confident in one's body.

Healing the root chakra can support your ability to feel safe in intimate situations, reduce sexual anxieties, and improve your overall sense of sexual vitality.

Grounding Practices: Spend time in nature, walk barefoot on the earth, or practice grounding meditations to connect with the physical body.

Affirmations: "I embrace my sexuality with confidence."

Body Awareness: Engage in body-positive practices like mindful touch, gentle yoga, or breathing exercises to foster a deeper connection to your body.

2. Sacral Chakra (Svadhisthana): Creativity, Pleasure, and Sexual Expression

Role of the Sacral Chakra in Sexual Healing: The sacral chakra is directly tied to sexual energy, pleasure, and emotional intimacy. It is the center of creativity, desire, and the ability to experience pleasure, including sexual pleasure. This chakra governs how we relate to our emotions, creativity, and sensuality.

Blockages in the sacral chakra often result in difficulty expressing or experiencing pleasure, emotional numbness, or shame around sexuality. It can also manifest as sexual repression, guilt, or a lack of desire.

Healing the sacral chakra restores the natural flow of sexual energy, allowing for healthy emotional and sexual expression.

Creative Expression: Engage in activities that foster creativity, such as dancing, painting, or writing, to open up the flow of sexual energy.

Pleasure Practices: Explore what brings you pleasure, both alone and with a partner. Sensual self-care rituals, like massage or a warm bath, can stimulate energy flow.

Affirmations: "I honor my body and its needs."

Sacral Chakra Yoga: Poses like hip openers (e.g., Pigeon Pose or Butterfly Pose) can release tension in the sacral region and enhance sexual energy.

3. Solar Plexus Chakra (Manipura): Confidence and Sexual Empowerment

Role of the Solar Plexus Chakra in Sexual Healing: The solar plexus chakra is the center of personal power, self-esteem, and confidence. It governs how we assert ourselves, set boundaries, and feel in control of our lives. In terms of sexual healing, this chakra influences how confident and empowered we feel in intimate situations.

When the solar plexus is out of balance, you may experience low self-esteem, fear of rejection, or difficulty asserting your sexual boundaries. This can lead to sexual disempowerment, feelings of inadequacy, or a lack of control over sexual experiences.

Healing the solar plexus chakra can boost self-confidence, making you feel empowered in your sexual expression and interactions.

Empowerment Practices: Engage in activities that increase your sense of self-worth, such as setting and achieving small personal goals, or speaking affirmations of empowerment.

Affirmations: "I honor my desires and feel empowered in my body."

Core Strengthening Exercises: Yoga poses such as Warrior II, Boat Pose, or Plank can help activate the solar plexus and reinforce your sense of personal power.

4. Heart Chakra (Anahata): Emotional Healing and Loving Sexuality

Role of the Heart Chakra in Sexual Healing: The heart chakra is the center of love, compassion, and emotional connection. It governs our ability to give and receive love, not just romantically, but also within ourselves and with others. In terms of sexual healing, a balanced heart chakra helps us cultivate loving, compassionate relationships, which are key to sexual experiences.

Blockages in the heart chakra can lead to emotional coldness, difficulty with vulnerability, or a lack of trust in sexual relationships. It can also cause emotional wounds from past experiences, such as heartbreak or betrayal, which may affect sexual intimacy.

Healing the heart chakra promotes unconditional love, empathy, and emotional healing, leading to a more profound, compassionate, and connected sexual experience.

Forgiveness: Work on forgiving past emotional wounds or experiences that may be affecting your sexual relationships. Journaling or talking about emotional hurts can help process them.

Affirmations: "I am open to love, and I trust love."

Heart-Opening Yoga: Poses like Camel Pose, Cobra Pose, and Bridge Pose open the chest and promote emotional release and healing.

5. Throat Chakra (Vishuddha): Communication and Sexual Expression

Role of the Throat Chakra in Sexual Healing: The throat chakra governs communication, both verbal and non-verbal. In terms of sexual healing, the throat chakra allows us to express our desires, boundaries, and emotions clearly and authentically.

Blockages in the throat chakra can lead to difficulties in expressing sexual needs or desires, leading to frustration or misunderstandings with partners. It can also result in feeling silenced or unheard in intimate situations.

Healing the throat chakra improves communication in sexual relationships, making it easier to express what you want and need in a healthy, respectful way.

Verbal Expression: Practice expressing your sexual desires and boundaries openly and honestly. Speaking affirmations of self-worth can also help break down barriers.

Affirmations: "I speak my truth with confidence and clarity."

Breathing Exercises: Practice deep, conscious breathing to relax the throat area and encourage the free flow of communication and expression.

6. Third Eye Chakra (Ajna): Intuition and Emotional Clarity in Sexuality

Role of the Third Eye Chakra in Sexual Healing:The third eye chakra is associated with intuition, inner wisdom, and mental clarity. In sexual healing, the third eye chakra helps you tune into your deepest desires, emotional needs, and the energetic dynamics in intimate relationships.

Blockages in the third eye chakra can lead to confusion about your sexual needs or a lack of clarity about what you desire. It may also cause difficulty in trusting your intuition in relationships.

Healing the third eye chakra fosters a deeper connection to your inner wisdom, helping you make decisions that align with your authentic sexual and emotional needs.

Meditation for Clarity: Meditation or mindfulness exercises can help you tune into your body and emotions, gaining insight into what you truly want in intimate experiences.

Affirmations: "I trust my intuition and inner wisdom."

Visualization: Visualize yourself in intimate moments where you feel aligned with your desires and emotionally fulfilled.

7. Crown Chakra (Sahasrara): Spiritual Connection and Sacred Sexuality

Role of the Crown Chakra in Sexual Healing: The crown chakra is associated with spiritual connection, enlightenment, and transcendence. In sexual healing, the crown chakra governs how connected we feel to something greater than ourselves and how sacred our sexuality is.

Blockages in the crown chakra can cause feelings of disconnection, isolation, or a lack of spiritual fulfillment in sexuality. It may also prevent you from experiencing sexual intimacy as a spiritual or sacred union.

Healing the crown chakra helps you experience sexuality as a divine and transcendent connection, allowing for deeper spiritual fulfillment and intimacy.

Spiritual Practices: Engage in spiritual practices such as prayer, meditation, or sacred rituals that honor your sexual energy as a sacred gift.

Affirmations: "I am connected to the divine energy of the universe."

Stillness and Presence: Engage in mindful, present sexual experiences where you allow yourself to be fully immersed in the moment, connecting on a spiritual level.

Shortcut for Sexual Healing: Accept sexuality is sacred.

CHAPTER XVII

CHAKRAS AND FINANCIAL HEALING

The connection between chakras and financial healing is grounded in the belief that our energy centers influence not only our emotional, physical, and spiritual well-being, but also our material experiences, including finances. When chakras are balanced and flowing harmoniously, we can experience abundance, financial security, and a healthy relationship with money. Conversely, when chakras are blocked or imbalanced, they can manifest as financial struggles, limiting beliefs around wealth, and challenges in attracting prosperity.

1. Root Chakra (Muladhara): Stability, Security, and Financial Foundation

Role of the Root Chakra in Financial Healing: The root chakra governs your sense of safety, stability, and connection to the earth. It is the foundation of your physical existence and your ability to feel secure in your material world. This chakra plays a significant role in your relationship to money, financial security, and the ability to provide for yourself.

When the root chakra is balanced, you feel secure, grounded, and confident in your ability to meet your financial needs. However, if the root chakra is imbalanced, it can lead to fears about survival, scarcity, and financial instability, which can block the flow of money into your life.

Financial difficulties, insecurity, and constant worry about money are often related to blockages in the root chakra.

Grounding Practices: Spend time in nature, walk barefoot on the earth, or engage in grounding exercises to help reconnect with the present moment and cultivate a sense of stability.

Affirmations: "I am safe. Money flows easily and effortlessly into my life."

Root Chakra Meditation: Visualize red light or energy flowing into your root chakra, grounding you and strengthening your sense of financial stability.

2. Sacral Chakra (Svadhisthana): Creative Flow and Prosperity

Role of the Sacral Chakra in Financial Healing: The sacral chakra governs creativity, pleasure, and the ability to experience emotional and material abundance. This chakra is associated with your capacity to manifest desires, including financial ones, by allowing creative energy to flow freely. It is also linked to how you value yourself and your work, which affects your ability to charge what you're worth.

When this chakra is balanced, you can manifest financial abundance through creativity, passion, and the ability to enjoy life's pleasures. However, blockages can lead to a feeling of creative stagnation, guilt around money, or difficulty receiving financial rewards for your efforts.

Creative Expression: Engage in activities that allow you to express your creativity, such as painting, writing, or brainstorming new ideas. Creative flow can often unlock financial flow as well.

Affirmations: "I am deserving of financial abundance and the fruits of my creativity."

Sacral Chakra Yoga: Practice hip-opening poses like Pigeon Pose or Butterfly Pose to release emotional blocks and stimulate the flow of creative energy, which can also translate into financial creativity.

3. Solar Plexus Chakra (Manipura): Personal Power and Financial Confidence

Role of the Solar Plexus Chakra in Financial Healing: The solar plexus chakra governs self-esteem, personal power, and confidence. It influences how we assert ourselves in the world, including in financial matters. This chakra plays a key role in our ability to take charge of our financial destiny, make empowered decisions, and feel confident in our capacity to create wealth.

A balanced solar plexus chakra allows you to set healthy boundaries, assert your value, and make wise financial choices.

When it is imbalanced, you may struggle with feelings of powerlessness, low self-worth, or fear of failure, which can hinder financial success.

Empowerment Practices: Engage in activities that build your self-confidence, such as setting financial goals, taking small steps toward financial independence, or practicing public speaking or negotiation skills.

Affirmations: "I am worthy of abundance."

Core Strengthening Yoga: Practice poses like Warrior II, Boat Pose, and Plank to activate your personal power and strengthen your ability to manifest financial success.

4. Heart Chakra (Anahata): Abundance, Generosity, and Financial Flow

Role of the Heart Chakra in Financial Healing:

The heart chakra is the center of love, compassion, and generosity. It governs our relationship to giving and receiving, including financial abundance. A healthy heart chakra promotes feelings of generosity, gratitude, and the ability to share resources, which can open the flow of wealth into your life.

When the heart chakra is blocked or imbalanced, you may experience feelings of lack, possessiveness, or scarcity, which can create barriers to financial flow. Conversely, an open and balanced heart chakra allows money to flow freely both in and out, as you feel comfortable receiving and giving.

Generosity Practices: Cultivate a mindset of abundance by donating time, money, or resources to others. Giving not only helps others, but it also creates a flow of positive energy that can return to you in the form of financial rewards.

Affirmations: "I trust the universe to provides for me and my loved ones."

Heart-Opening Yoga: Practice poses such as Camel Pose or Cobra Pose to open the chest and heart, releasing blocks to love and abundance.

5. Throat Chakra (Vishuddha): Communication and Financial Expression

Role of the Throat Chakra in Financial Healing: The throat chakra governs communication, self-expression, and the ability to speak your truth. This chakra influences your capacity to express your financial needs, desires, and boundaries. Clear communication around money and financial matters is essential for building wealth and maintaining financial health.

Blockages in the throat chakra can lead to difficulty in negotiating financial terms, asking for raises, or even feeling embarrassed to talk about money. It can also manifest as a fear of expressing financial goals or standing up for your value in financial negotiations.

Effective Communication: Practice articulating your financial needs and desires clearly, whether it's negotiating a salary, discussing investments, or setting financial boundaries.

Affirmations: "I communicate my financial needs with ease and integrity."

Breathwork and Vocal Expression: Deep breathing exercises and chanting can help clear blockages in the throat chakra, allowing you to express yourself more freely, particularly in financial matters.

6. Third Eye Chakra (Ajna): Clarity, Intuition, and Financial Decision Making

Role of the Third Eye Chakra in Financial Healing: The third eye chakra is associated with intuition, inner wisdom, and mental clarity. It plays an important role in your ability to make sound financial decisions, trust your gut feelings, and foresee financial opportunities. The third eye chakra helps you see beyond the obvious, allowing you to make strategic investments and financial choices based on deeper insight.

When the third eye chakra is blocked, you may experience confusion around financial matters, difficulty making decisions, or a lack of trust in your intuition. Financial decisions may feel unclear or challenging, leading to fear-based choices.

Intuitive Decision-Making: Practice tapping into your intuition by meditating on financial choices and trusting your gut feelings. Keep a journal to track your intuitive insights related to finances.

Affirmations: "I make clear, confident financial decisions."

Visualization: Visualize yourself achieving financial success and clarity in your financial decisions. This can help create mental alignment with your financial goals.

7. Crown Chakra (Sahasrara): Spiritual Connection and Prosperity

Role of the Crown Chakra in Financial Healing: The crown chakra is linked to spiritual connection, enlightenment, and the understanding of universal abundance. It governs your ability to feel connected to the larger flow of life and trust that the universe provides. When balanced, the crown chakra fosters a mindset of divine prosperity, helping you align with the idea that abundance is your birthright.

Blockages in the crown chakra can cause feelings of disconnection or a lack of trust in the universe's ability to provide for you, creating financial scarcity or lack of inspiration to manifest wealth.

Spiritual Practices: Engage in spiritual practices that reinforce your belief in abundance and your connection to a higher source, such as meditation, prayer, or gratitude practices.

Affirmations: "I am connected to the infinite abundance of the universe."

Mindfulness and Presence: Practice being present and grateful for the abundance you currently have, which opens up the energy channels for more prosperity to flow.

Holistic Financial Healing Practices

Chakra Meditation: Meditate on each chakra individually, visualizing the colors associated with each chakra (e.g., red for the root, orange for the sacral, etc.) and focusing on how the energy flows through you. Use this practice to release blockages related to money and abundance.

Energy Healing: Techniques like energy healing, sound healing, or crystal healing can help clear blockages in the chakras and allow financial energy to flow more freely.

Mindset Shifts: Alongside chakra healing practices, work on shifting limiting beliefs around money. This might include challenging the notion that money is scarce or that you are unworthy of financial abundance.

Shortcut for Financial Healing: Modesty and Humility.

CHAPTER XVIII

CHAKRAS AND SPIRITUAL HEALING

Chakras play a crucial role in spiritual healing, as they are the energy centers that govern not only our physical and emotional well-being but also our spiritual connection and growth. When the chakras are balanced, they help facilitate a deeper connection to our higher selves, the divine, and the universal flow of energy. When imbalanced or blocked, they can hinder spiritual growth, leading to feelings of disconnect, confusion, or stagnation on a spiritual path.

1. Root Chakra (Muladhara): Grounding and Connection to Earth

Role in Spiritual Healing: The root chakra is your foundation, grounding you in the physical world. In spiritual terms, it connects you to the Earth, helping you feel supported and anchored in your body and the material world. A balanced root chakra provides the stability you need to explore spiritual realms, as it keeps you grounded and secure.

When the root chakra is blocked, you may feel disconnected from your physical body, unsafe in the world, or spiritually adrift. In these cases, spiritual growth may feel unattainable or disconnected from practical realities.

Healing the root chakra allows you to feel a sense of security and belonging in the universe, which is essential for further spiritual exploration.

Grounding Practices: Spend time outdoors, practice mindfulness, or walk barefoot to reconnect with the Earth. Visualize roots extending from your body into the ground.

Affirmations: "I am safe, secure, and supported by the Earth."

Earth-Based Rituals: Perform grounding rituals, such as lighting a red candle or holding crystals like hematite or red jasper, to strengthen the root chakra and deepen your spiritual connection.

2. Sacral Chakra (Svadhisthana): Creativity, Pleasure, and Emotional Balance

Role in Spiritual Healing: The sacral chakra governs creativity, emotional well-being, and our connection to pleasure and joy. Spiritually, it is related to the flow of energy, both in our physical body and in our spiritual practices. A balanced sacral chakra enhances your ability to connect to spiritual experiences through creative expression and emotional openness.

Blockages in the sacral chakra can cause emotional numbness, creative blocks, or guilt around receiving pleasure. This may impede spiritual practices, especially those requiring emotional or creative openness.

Healing the sacral chakra facilitates the free flow of spiritual energy and emotional clarity, allowing you to experience divine creativity and spiritual joy.

Creative Expression: Engage in art, dance, or any form of creative activity that allows your spiritual energy to flow.

Affirmations: "I honor my emotions as sacred."

Sacral Chakra Meditation: Visualize orange light filling your sacral chakra, releasing emotional blocks and allowing the creative flow of energy to connect you to your spiritual essence.

3. Solar Plexus Chakra (Manipura): Personal Power and Spiritual Confidence

Role in Spiritual Healing: The solar plexus chakra is the seat of personal power, confidence, and will. Spiritually, it governs how we assert ourselves in the world, set our intentions, and trust our inner guidance. A balanced solar plexus chakra enhances your ability to trust your inner wisdom and your spiritual power, giving you the confidence to step into your full spiritual potential.

If this chakra is blocked, it can result in feelings of powerlessness, self-doubt, or confusion about one's purpose. This can create barriers to spiritual growth as you may feel incapable of following your spiritual path or manifesting your divine purpose.

Healing the solar plexus chakra allows you to embrace your spiritual empowerment and take aligned actions that lead to your higher purpose.

Confidence-Building Practices: Set spiritual goals, make decisions aligned with your intuition, and trust your inner guidance.

Affirmations: "I am confident in my spiritual path."

Solar Plexus Yoga: Practice core-strengthening poses such as Boat Pose, Warrior II, and Plank to activate personal power and boost spiritual confidence.

4. Heart Chakra (Anahata): Love, Compassion, and Divine Connection

Role in Spiritual Healing: The heart chakra is the center of love, compassion, and emotional healing. It governs how we connect with others and ourselves on a deep, spiritual level. In spiritual healing, the heart chakra is essential for experiencing unconditional love, both for yourself and the world around you.

A blocked or unbalanced heart chakra can cause emotional wounds, difficulty giving or receiving love, and a sense of spiritual isolation. You may feel disconnected from your soul's purpose or struggle with forgiveness.

Healing the heart chakra opens you to divine love, allowing you to experience greater spiritual connection and alignment with universal love and compassion.

Self-Love Practices: Engage in self-compassionate rituals like affirmations, self-care, and meditation on love.

Affirmations: "I trust in the healing power of unconditional love."

Heart-Opening Yoga: Poses such as Camel Pose, Cobra Pose, or Bridge Pose help to open the chest and heart, releasing emotional blockages and allowing the free flow of spiritual energy.

5. Throat Chakra (Vishuddha): Truth, Expression, and Spiritual Communication

Role in Spiritual Healing: The throat chakra governs communication, self-expression, and the ability to speak your truth. Spiritually, it allows you to express your inner wisdom, communicate with the divine, and align your words with your higher purpose. This chakra is vital for speaking spiritual truths and manifesting your soul's intentions through clear expression.

A blocked throat chakra can create difficulties in expressing yourself authentically, leading to a sense of spiritual repression or a lack of clarity about your spiritual path.

Healing the throat chakra enhances your ability to communicate with spiritual beings, your higher self, and the universe, facilitating the expression of your true spiritual voice.

Verbal Expression: Practice speaking your truth in all areas of your life, both in daily conversations and in your spiritual practice.

Affirmations: "I trust my voice and spiritual expression."

Throat Chakra Meditation: Focus on breathing exercises or chanting mantras that resonate with the throat chakra, such as "Ham," to enhance spiritual communication.

6. Third Eye Chakra (Ajna): Intuition, Insight, and Spiritual Vision

Role in Spiritual Healing: The third eye chakra governs intuition, insight, and spiritual vision. It allows you to see beyond the physical realm and access deeper spiritual knowledge, divine guidance, and higher consciousness. This chakra is central to perceiving spiritual truths and gaining clarity on your spiritual journey.

Blockages in the third eye chakra can result in confusion, lack of direction, or an inability to trust your intuition. You may feel spiritually lost or disconnected from your inner wisdom.

Healing the third eye chakra enhances your ability to receive spiritual insights, visions, and guidance, which helps you align with your soul's path and divine purpose.

Intuition Practices: Engage in meditation or practices that help you tune into your intuition, such as journaling, dream work, or divination tools like tarot.

Affirmations: "I trust my intuition and spiritual vision."

Third Eye Meditation: Focus on the space between your eyebrows and visualize indigo or purple light radiating from the area to enhance clarity and spiritual insight.

7. Crown Chakra (Sahasrara): Spiritual Enlightenment and Divine Connection

Role in Spiritual Healing: The crown chakra is the center of spiritual enlightenment, divine connection, and universal consciousness. It governs your connection to the divine, higher realms, and the understanding of universal truth. This chakra represents the culmination of spiritual awakening and the realization of your oneness with the universe.

When the crown chakra is blocked or imbalanced, you may feel spiritually disconnected, isolated, or unsure of your higher purpose. This can prevent you from accessing higher spiritual wisdom or experiencing profound enlightenment.

Healing the crown chakra opens you to the flow of divine energy, allowing you to experience a deeper connection to the universe and spiritual oneness.

Meditation: Engage in deep, stillness-focused meditation to open the crown chakra and receive spiritual insights.

Affirmations: "I am one with the divinet."

Crown Chakra Visualization: Visualize violet or white light flowing into the top of your head, connecting you to divine consciousness and spiritual awakening.

Shortcut for Spiritual Healing: Praying, Meditating, Observing your thoughts.

CHAPTER XIX

CHAKRAS AND GOOD HEALTH

The chakras, as centers of energy in the body, play a crucial role in maintaining overall health, as they are believed to govern both physical and mental well-being. When the chakras are balanced and enegy flowing freely, the body and mind function optimally. However, when these energy centers are blocked or imbalanced, it can manifest in physical, emotional, or mental health issues. Each chakra is linked to specific organs and bodily systems, and by understanding this connection, we can work on promoting good health through chakra healing.

Each chakra governs specific areas of the body, mind, and spirit. When these energy centers are aligned, they support your physical health, emotional well-being, mental clarity, and spiritual growth. Embrace practices like yoga, meditation, breathing exercises, and affirmations to maintain chakra balance and promote optimal health.

1. Root Chakra (Muladhara) and Good Health

The Root Chakra, located at the base of the spine, is directly related to the physical body's foundational health. It governs the skeletal system, the adrenal glands, and the legs and feet. It is also linked to survival instincts, safety, and security. When this chakra is balanced, you feel physically grounded, secure, and healthy. If it's imbalanced, it can lead to issues with the lower body, such as problems with the legs, feet, lower back, or digestive system.

Physical Body: The Root Chakra influences the health of the bones, teeth, legs, feet, and large intestines. Imbalances in this chakra can manifest as chronic lower back pain, leg or knee problems, or issues with bowel function.

Adrenal Glands: This chakra regulates the adrenal glands, which are responsible for the "fight or flight" response. If the Root Chakra is underactive, you may feel fatigued or experience chronic stress.

Grounding Exercises: Practice grounding techniques, such as walking barefoot on grass or soil, to enhance physical health.

Physical Exercise: Regular exercise that involves the lower body, like walking, yoga (especially poses like Mountain Pose or Warrior Pose), and strength training, can help open the Root Chakra.

Healthy Diet: A balanced diet rich in protein, root vegetables, and grounding foods, such as beets, carrots, and potatoes, can support the Root Chakra.

Affirmations: "I am healthy, strong, stable, and grounded."

2. Sacral Chakra (Svadhisthana) and Good Health

The Sacral Chakra, located just below the navel, governs the reproductive system, kidneys, bladder, and the lower digestive system. It is also the energy center for creativity, pleasure, and emotional balance. This chakra directly influences sexual health and emotional well-being. A balanced Sacral Chakra promotes healthy relationships, emotional stability, and reproductive health.

Reproductive System: The Sacral Chakra governs sexual health, fertility, and reproductive organs. Imbalances may result in sexual dysfunction, menstrual issues, infertility, or urinary problems.

Kidneys and Bladder: The Sacral Chakra also influences the kidneys, bladder, and lower digestive system. Imbalances can manifest as kidney infections, bladder problems, or digestive disorders.

Creative Expression: Engage in creative activities like painting, dancing, or writing to stimulate the Sacral Chakra and improve emotional health.

Yoga Poses: Hip-opening poses like Pigeon Pose or Butterfly Pose can help release tension and energy blockages in the Sacral Chakra.

Hydration: Drink plenty of water and consume foods with high water content, such as fruits and vegetables, to support the Sacral Chakra's connection to the kidneys and bladder.

Affirmations: " I am healthy, balanced, and at peace with my emotions."

3. Solar Plexus Chakra (Manipura) and Good Health

The Solar Plexus Chakra, located just above the navel, is associated with the digestive system, metabolism, and energy production. It governs the stomach, liver, pancreas, and intestines. This chakra is linked to personal power, self-esteem, and the ability to take action. A balanced Solar Plexus Chakra helps maintain a healthy digestive system and regulates metabolism.

Digestive System: The Solar Plexus Chakra is closely linked to the stomach, liver, pancreas, and small intestine. Imbalances in this chakra may lead to digestive issues like indigestion, ulcers, acid reflux, or liver problems.

Energy Levels: The Solar Plexus also governs our energy levels. When it is imbalanced, you may feel lethargic, lack motivation, or experience fatigue.

Core Strengthening: Engage in exercises that strengthen the core, such as Pilates, abdominal exercises, or poses like Boat Pose and Plank Pose.

Breathing Exercises: Practice deep breathing exercises like Pranayama to stimulate and activate the Solar Plexus Chakra.

Balanced Diet: A healthy diet rich in fiber, complex carbohydrates, and fresh vegetables will support digestive health and energy.

Affirmations: "I am powerful, confident, and in control of my life."

4. Heart Chakra (Anahata) and Good Health

The Heart Chakra governs the heart, lungs, and circulatory system. It is the center of love, compassion, and emotional balance. When balanced, it promotes cardiovascular health, emotional well-being, and overall vitality. The Heart Chakra also influences immune function and helps maintain healthy blood circulation.

Cardiovascular Health: The Heart Chakra is directly linked to heart health, the lungs, and the circulatory system. Blockages may result in conditions like heart disease, lung problems, or high blood pressure.

Immune System: A balanced Heart Chakra boosts the immune system, as it promotes emotional well-being and emotional release, both of which support physical health.

Heart-Opening Yoga: Practice heart-opening poses like Cobra Pose, Camel Pose, or Bridge Pose to release tension and enhance circulation.

Breathing Exercises: Deep breathing, particularly through the chest, can help open the Heart Chakra and promote circulation.

Emotional Healing: Address emotional wounds by practicing forgiveness and cultivating compassion toward yourself and others.

Affirmations: "I am open to love, compassion, and healing."

5. Throat Chakra (Vishuddha) and Good Health

The Throat Chakra governs the throat, thyroid, and respiratory system. It influences communication, self-expression, and the ability to speak one's truth. When the Throat Chakra is balanced, it supports clear and effective communication, as well as a healthy respiratory and thyroid system.

Throat and Respiratory Health: The Throat Chakra governs the throat, vocal cords, lungs, and respiratory system. Imbalances in this chakra can lead to throat infections, respiratory issues, hoarseness, or thyroid imbalances.

Thyroid Function: The Throat Chakra influences the thyroid, which regulates metabolism. Imbalances can result in hyperthyroidism, hypothyroidism, or other thyroid disorders.

Voice and Sound Healing: Use chanting, singing, or humming to activate and heal the Throat Chakra. Practice vocal exercises or engage in sound healing therapies like toning or listening to specific frequencies.

Breathing Exercises: Practice pranayama or deep breathing to cleanse and balance the throat and lungs.

Hydration: Stay hydrated and consume foods that support throat health, such as honey, warm teas, or herbal tonics.

Affirmations: "I express myself freely and clearly."

6. Third Eye Chakra (Ajna) and Good Health

The Third Eye Chakra is the center of intuition and mental clarity. It governs the brain, eyes, and nervous system. This chakra influences your ability to process information, stay mentally clear, and trust your intuition. When the Third Eye Chakra is balanced, you experience mental clarity, insight, and a deep sense of peace.

Brain and Nervous System: The Third Eye Chakra governs the brain, pituitary gland, and nervous system. Imbalances can manifest as headaches, eye problems, neurological issues, or mental confusion.

Mental Health: The Third Eye Chakra is also connected to the ability to think clearly and make sound decisions. Mental health conditions like anxiety or depression can arise from imbalances here.

Meditation: Meditation, particularly visualization or mindfulness practices, helps to open and balance the Third Eye Chakra.

Eye Exercises: Practice eye exercises, such as focusing on a single point or gazing softly into the distance to relax and strengthen the eye muscles.

Mindful Living: Engage in practices that enhance mental clarity, such as journaling, mindfulness, and intuitive exercises.

Affirmations: "I see the truth in all situations."

7. Crown Chakra (Sahasrara) and Good Health

The Crown Chakra is associated with spiritual connection, enlightenment, and the brain. It governs your ability to connect to higher consciousness, universal energy, and experience deep inner peace. When this chakra is balanced, it promotes mental health, spiritual well-being, and overall vitality.

Brain and Nervous System: The Crown Chakra governs the brain, pineal gland, and nervous system. Imbalances in this chakra can result in mental confusion, cognitive dysfunction, or sleep disturbances.

Spiritual Health: The Crown Chakra is connected to your spiritual state, and when it's balanced, you feel connected to the universe and experience peace.

Spiritual Practice: Engage in spiritual practices such as meditation, prayer, or connecting with nature to enhance the Crown Chakra.

Cleansing Rituals: Use rituals like sound healing or light therapy to cleanse and stimulate the Crown Chakra.

Mindfulness and Silence: Spend time in silence, focusing on your inner peace and spiritual growth.

Affirmations: "I am connected to the divine"

CHAPTER XX

CHAKRAS AND HAPPINESS

The chakras are intricately linked to various aspects of happiness, as each energy center governs different parts of the body, mind, and emotions. When our chakras are balanced and open, we are more likely to experience a sense of well-being, fulfillment, and joy. Conversely, imbalances or blockages in the chakras can hinder our ability to experience true happiness. By understanding how each chakra contributes to our overall happiness, we can use chakra work to enhance our mood, emotional resilience, and sense of inner peace. By nurturing and balancing each of the seven chakras, you create the conditions for lasting happiness.

1. Root Chakra (Muladhara) and Happiness

The Root Chakra is the foundation of our physical and emotional stability. It is located at the base of the spine and is associated with our sense of safety, security, and belonging. When the Root Chakra is balanced, we feel grounded and secure, which provides the emotional stability necessary for happiness. If this chakra is blocked or imbalanced, feelings of fear, insecurity, or instability can arise, hindering our ability to experience lasting happiness.

A balanced Root Chakra supports feelings of stability and safety, which are essential for mental and emotional well-being.

It encourages a sense of belonging and connection to the earth, fostering an inner peace that forms the basis for true happiness.

An imbalance may lead to anxiety, financial stress, or difficulty trusting others, which can prevent happiness from flourishing.

Grounding Exercises: Walking barefoot on the earth, gardening, or practicing grounding yoga poses like Mountain Pose can help stabilize the Root Chakra.

Affirmations: "I am safe, secure, and supported."

Connection to Nature: Spending time in nature, especially in natural settings like forests, parks, or the beach, can help activate the Root Chakra and improve feelings of safety and well-being.

2. Sacral Chakra (Svadhisthana) and Happiness

The Sacral Chakra, located just below the navel, governs our emotions, creativity, pleasure, and sexuality. It is deeply tied to our ability to enjoy life and experience happiness in the present moment. When the Sacral Chakra is balanced, we can embrace joy, pleasure, and creativity with ease. On the other hand, blockages in this chakra can lead to emotional numbness, difficulty experiencing pleasure, or challenges with self-expression.

This chakra fosters the ability to experience pleasure, joy, and emotional connection. A balanced Sacral Chakra allows us to fully enjoy life and create meaningful connections with others.

It is also the center of creativity, so when it is open, we are more likely to feel inspired and motivated, contributing to a greater sense of fulfillment and happiness.

An imbalance may manifest as emotional numbness, repressed desires, or difficulty in forming intimate connections.

Creative Expression: Engage in creative activities such as dancing, painting, writing, or any activity that allows you to express yourself freely and fully.

Yoga Poses: Hip-opening poses like Pigeon Pose or Butterfly Pose can help release emotional tension and activate the Sacral Chakra.

Affirmations: "I allow myself to feel fully alive."

Self-Care: Pamper yourself with activities that make you feel nurtured, such as a warm bath, massage, or indulging in a favorite hobby.

3. Solar Plexus Chakra (Manipura) and Happiness

The Solar Plexus Chakra, located above the navel, governs personal power, confidence, and self-esteem. It is closely tied to our sense of self-worth and our ability to take action in life. When the Solar Plexus Chakra is balanced, we feel confident, empowered, and motivated to pursue our goals. This sense of empowerment is key to achieving lasting happiness. An imbalance in this chakra can result in feelings of low self-esteem, lack of control, or inability to take initiative.

The Solar Plexus Chakra helps us take responsibility for our lives and our happiness. When this chakra is open, we are confident in our decisions and have the inner strength to pursue our goals.

It also relates to the ability to set boundaries and maintain healthy relationships, which contributes to our overall emotional well-being.

An imbalance may manifest as indecisiveness, low self-esteem, or feelings of powerlessness.

Core-Strengthening Exercises: Engage in exercises that strengthen your core, such as abdominal exercises, Pilates, or poses like Boat Pose or Plank Pose.

Affirmations: "I trust in my ability to create the life I desire."

Action-Oriented Practices: Take steps toward your goals, no matter how small. Every action taken boosts confidence and reinforces your personal power.

4. Heart Chakra (Anahata) and Happiness

The Heart Chakra, located at the center of the chest, is the seat of love, compassion, and emotional connection. It is the bridge between the lower physical chakras and the upper spiritual chakras. A balanced Heart Chakra allows us to give and receive love freely, creating a deep sense of emotional fulfillment and happiness. When this chakra is blocked, we may feel disconnected from others or unable to experience love, both of which hinder happiness.

The Heart Chakra is the center of love and compassion, both for oneself and others. When this chakra is balanced, it allows us to experience deep emotional fulfillment, joy, and connection with others.

It fosters empathy, kindness, and forgiveness, which are essential for cultivating happiness in relationships.

An imbalance in the Heart Chakra can lead to feelings of loneliness, grief, or difficulty in forming meaningful emotional connections.

Heart-Opening Yoga: Practice poses like Cobra Pose, Camel Pose, or Bridge Pose to open the chest and stimulate the Heart

Chakra.

Affirmations: "I am worthy of love."

Acts of Kindness: Engage in acts of kindness, whether small or large, to foster compassion and strengthen the emotional bonds that bring happiness.

5. Throat Chakra (Vishuddha) and Happiness

The Throat Chakra, located at the throat, governs communication, self-expression, and authenticity. It allows us to express our thoughts, feelings and desires clearly and truthfully. When the Throat Chakra is balanced, we can communicate our needs and desires openly, creating harmony in our relationships and reducing internal conflict. This authentic self-expression is key to experiencing happiness and fulfillment. Blockages in the Throat Chakra may result in difficulty expressing oneself or feeling misunderstood.

A balanced Throat Chakra allows for clear and authentic communication, which is vital for creating harmonious relationships and reducing stress or conflict.

It fosters the ability to speak your truth and be heard, which promotes emotional and mental well-being.

An imbalance in the Throat Chakra can lead to feelings of frustration, repression, or not being able to express oneself fully.

Voice and Sound Healing: Engage in practices that activate the Throat Chakra, such as chanting, singing, or humming.

Affirmations: "I communicate with confidence."

Writing and Journaling: Write your thoughts and feelings in a journal or create art that expresses your inner truth.

6. Third Eye Chakra (Ajna) and Happiness

The Third Eye Chakra, located between the eyebrows, is the center of intuition, wisdom, and mental clarity. It governs our ability to see beyond the surface, access higher wisdom, and trust our inner guidance. A balanced Third Eye Chakra helps us make decisions that align with our true desires and values, leading to greater contentment and happiness. When this chakra is imbalanced, we may experience confusion, lack of direction, or an inability to trust our intuition.

The Third Eye Chakra promotes mental clarity, insight, and intuition. When it is open, we are able to make decisions that are aligned with our true self, leading to greater happiness.

It also enhances our ability to perceive the deeper meanings of life, which fosters a sense of purpose and fulfillment.

An imbalance may lead to confusion, lack of direction, or difficulty trusting one's intuition.

Meditation: Practice meditation, particularly visualization or mindfulness, to activate the Third Eye Chakra and cultivate mental clarity.

Affirmations: "I see life with clarity and insight."

Mindful Living: Engage in practices that enhance awareness, such as mindful eating, walking, or deep listening.

7. Crown Chakra (Sahasrara) and Happiness

The Crown Chakra, located at the top of the head, governs our spiritual connection and sense of oneness with the universe. It is associated with higher consciousness, enlightenment, and inner peace. When the Crown Chakra is balanced, we feel a deep sense of spiritual fulfillment and connection, which leads to lasting happiness. Imbalances in this chakra can lead to feelings of isolation, lack of purpose, or spiritual disconnection.

The Crown Chakra fosters spiritual connection and inner peace, which are key components of true happiness.

A balanced Crown Chakra helps us feel a sense of purpose and alignment with the universe, providing the foundation for emotional and spiritual well-being.

An imbalance may lead to feelings of isolation, a lack of purpose, or disconnection from the divine.

Spiritual Practice: Engage in spiritual practices such as prayer, meditation, or connecting with nature to enhance the Crown Chakra.

Affirmations: "I am one with the universe."

Silence and Stillness: Spend time in silence, cultivating inner stillness and connection to the divine.

CHAPTER XXI

CHAKRAS AND PROSPERITY

The connection between chakras and prosperity is deeply rooted in both spiritual and material realms. Prosperity, in this context, isn't just about financial wealth but extends to abundance in all aspects of life, such as health, relationships, personal fulfillment, and spiritual growth. Prosperity is often blocked or limited by imbalances in the energy centers (chakras), and aligning them can help open the flow of abundance and manifestation. By focusing on each chakra's unique contribution to prosperity—whether it's security, creativity, willpower, love, communication, vision, or divine connection—you can align your energy and mindset to manifest abundance in your life.

1. Root Chakra (Muladhara) and Prosperity

The Root Chakra is the foundation of your physical and material existence. It governs your sense of security, stability, and survival. A well-balanced Root Chakra allows you to feel safe and secure in your environment, which is necessary for attracting abundance. When the Root Chakra is strong, you feel grounded and supported by the universe, which translates into financial stability and the confidence to create and nurture prosperity.

Security: Feeling safe and secure allows you to take the necessary steps to build wealth, take risks, and make confident decisions. A balanced Root Chakra nurtures self-confidence, which directly impacts your ability to achieve financial success.

Abundance of Resources: The Root Chakra is linked to the flow of material resources and basic needs. When balanced, it attracts wealth and ensures that your basic survival needs are met, which is the foundation for long-term prosperity.

Grounding Energy: If you feel ungrounded or unstable, prosperity will be hard to manifest. Practices like spending time in nature, walking barefoot on the earth, or meditating can help ground the Root Chakra

Affirmations: "I am safe, supported, and secure."

Physical Activity: Activities like walking, running, dancing, or yoga poses like Mountain Pose or Tree Pose can help balance the Root Chakra.

Red Jasper or Hematite Crystals: These grounding stones can help promote security and stability.

2. Sacral Chakra (Svadhisthana) and Prosperity

The Sacral Chakra governs creativity, sensuality, emotions, and the ability to enjoy life's pleasures. Prosperity isn't just about money; it also involves creative expression and emotional fulfillment. The Sacral Chakra is directly tied to the ability to receive and enjoy abundance, and it allows you to experience the flow of prosperity in both tangible and intangible ways.

Creativity: When the Sacral Chakra is balanced, you are more in touch with your creative self. Creativity drives innovation, entrepreneurship, and unique problem-solving, all of which lead to new opportunities and success.

Openness to Pleasure: Prosperity isn't just about material wealth but about the abundance of joy, pleasure, and emotional fulfillment. A healthy Sacral Chakra allows you to receive these gifts and appreciate life's pleasures.

Healthy Relationships: Prosperity also involves healthy, abundant relationships. When the Sacral Chakra is open, it enhances your ability to form meaningful, supportive connections with others, which often leads to shared wealth, success, and prosperity.

Affirmations: "I deserve abundance."

Creative Expression: Engage in activities like painting, dancing, writing, or any other creative outlet that excites you and brings joy.

Orange Stones or Carnelian Crystals: These are linked with the Sacral Chakra and can help stimulate creative energy and the flow of abundance.

3. Solar Plexus Chakra (Manipura) and Prosperity

The Solar Plexus Chakra is the center of personal power, will, and self-confidence. It is directly linked to your ability to manifest prosperity in the material world. This chakra gives you the confidence to take action, overcome obstacles, and achieve your goals. A balanced Solar Plexus Chakra allows you to trust your own power and take inspired action toward wealth and success.

Self-Confidence and Willpower: The Solar Plexus Chakra fuels your self-esteem and personal power. When it is balanced, you are confident in your abilities and feel empowered to create wealth and success.

Goal-Setting and Action: This chakra helps you set clear goals and take consistent action to achieve them. It is the energy center that helps you stay focused and disciplined on your journey to prosperity.

Manifestation Power: The Solar Plexus is also a vital chakra for manifestation. When open, it helps you tap into the energy of the universe and the force of your own will to bring about the abundance you desire.

Affirmations: "I am worthy of success."

Action and Discipline: Take practical steps towards your goals. Start small, and take consistent action every day to build your prosperity.

Yellow Stones or Citrine Crystals: Citrine is known as the “merchant’s stone” and is associated with attracting wealth and abundance.

4. Heart Chakra (Anahata) and Prosperity

The Heart Chakra is the center of love, compassion, and connection to others. Prosperity is not just about material wealth, but the abundance of love, kindness, and support from others. When the Heart Chakra is open, you attract not only material wealth but also the energy of love, generosity, and emotional fulfillment.

Attracting Abundance Through Love: Prosperity often comes when we give and receive love. A balanced Heart Chakra allows you to attract love from all directions—love from family, friends, and community, which can open doors to prosperity in all areas of life.

Generosity and Gratitude: Prosperity is a flow of energy, and when we are generous with our time, resources, and love, we invite abundance into our lives. The Heart Chakra encourages us to give freely without fear of loss.

Emotional Fulfillment: Prosperity is not just about financial wealth but about emotional richness. A healthy Heart Chakra allows you to create emotional abundance by maintaining healthy relationships and nurturing positive, supportive emotional states.

Affirmations: "I am open to love and abundance."

Acts of Kindness: Practice generosity and show love to those around you.

Green Stones or Rose Quartz Crystals: Rose Quartz is known for attracting love, while Green Aventurine is associated with abundance and luck.

5. Throat Chakra (Vishuddha) and Prosperity

The Throat Chakra governs communication and self-expression. Prosperity, particularly in the form of career success, business ventures, and social abundance, is linked to your ability to express yourself clearly and authentically. When the Throat Chakra is balanced, it supports your ability to communicate your needs, desires, and ideas effectively, attracting prosperity through clear, authentic expression.

Clear Communication: Effective communication is essential for success in business, relationships, and personal endeavors. The Throat Chakra allows you to speak your truth and express your needs, which attracts prosperity through aligned actions and conversations.

Networking and Social Connections: The Throat Chakra helps you connect with others and build relationships that can open doors to opportunities. Prosperity often comes from strong, supportive networks and collaborations.

Creative Expression: Prosperity is also nurtured through creative expression. Whether it's through writing, speaking, or artistic endeavors, the Throat Chakra helps manifest abundance through communication and creativity.

Affirmations: "I speak my truth with confidence and clarity."

Public Speaking or Singing: Engage in practices that involve speaking or singing, such as giving a speech or singing in a group, to open up the Throat Chakra.

Blue Stones or Aquamarine Crystals: Aquamarine enhances communication, self-expression, and creativity.

6. Third Eye Chakra (Ajna) and Prosperity

The Third Eye Chakra is linked to intuition, vision, and insight. Prosperity is often attracted through vision—seeing opportunities and recognizing potential. The Third Eye helps you tap into your intuitive wisdom to make decisions that lead to success, allowing you to understand the bigger picture and align your actions accordingly.

Intuitive Decision-Making: Prosperity is not always about logical decisions but often about trusting your intuition. The Third Eye Chakra helps you see beyond the surface, guiding you toward opportunities and choices that lead to success.

Vision and Clarity: The ability to envision your goals and take inspired action is a key element of prosperity. The Third Eye enhances your capacity to visualize your future and set clear intentions for success.

Perception of Opportunities: This chakra sharpens your perception, allowing you to see opportunities that might otherwise be hidden, helping you create wealth and abundance.

Affirmations: "I see opportunities clearly."

Meditation and Visualization: Practice mindfulness and visualization techniques to strengthen the Third Eye's power to guide you.

Indigo Stones or Amethyst Crystals: Amethyst enhances intuition and spiritual insight.

7. Crown Chakra (Sahasrara) and Prosperity

The Crown Chakra is the gateway to spiritual wisdom and divine connection. True prosperity, according to many spiritual traditions, involves aligning with the divine flow of the universe. The Crown

Chakra helps you connect to your higher self and to the universal energy of abundance.

Divine Guidance: Prosperity can be guided by spiritual principles. The Crown Chakra helps you connect to the divine source of all abundance, offering wisdom and guidance in your pursuit of prosperity.

Unity with the Universe: True prosperity comes from understanding your interconnectedness with the world. A balanced Crown Chakra fosters a deep sense of spiritual fulfillment and alignment with the universe's abundant flow.

Affirmations: "I am connected to the infinite abundance of the universe."

Spiritual Practices: Meditation, prayer, or deep reflection can help open the Crown Chakra.

Clear Quartz or Amethyst Crystals: Clear Quartz helps amplify spiritual connections and divine guidance.

CHAPTER XXII

CHAKRAS AND PEACE

The chakras, as centers of energy in the body, play a crucial role in fostering inner peace. Peace is not merely the absence of conflict but a state of balance, harmony, and alignment in all aspects of life—physical, emotional, mental, and spiritual. Each chakra governs different aspects of our being, and when they are balanced, they create a sense of inner peace that transcends external circumstances. Understanding how each chakra influences peace can help you cultivate a more peaceful existence. When your chakras are aligned, you are better able to navigate life with calm, clarity, and acceptance, ultimately leading to a profound sense of inner peace.

1. Root Chakra (Muladhara) and Peace

The Root Chakra is the foundation of the chakra system and governs our sense of safety, stability, and grounding. When this chakra is balanced, we feel secure and connected to the Earth, which is essential for experiencing peace. The Root Chakra helps us feel that we belong and are supported by the world around us, reducing fear and anxiety.

Grounding and Security: A balanced Root Chakra gives you a sense of physical and emotional security. When we feel safe and supported, it's easier to remain calm and peaceful, regardless of external circumstances.

Overcoming Fear: Fear is a significant barrier to peace. A blocked Root Chakra can make us feel anxious and fearful. When this chakra is open, it helps us release these fears and accept the present moment.

Connection to the Earth: The Root Chakra connects us to the grounding energy of the Earth, helping to stabilize us during stressful time.

Affirmations: "I am safe, secure, and grounded."

Grounding Techniques: Practice walking barefoot on the earth, gardening, or sitting in nature. Yoga poses like Mountain Pose and Tree Pose are also effective for grounding.

Crystals: Hematite, Black Tourmaline, and Red Jasper support grounding and calming energies.

2. Sacral Chakra (Svadhisthana) and Peace

The Sacral Chakra is associated with emotions, creativity, and pleasure. When it is balanced, we can experience emotional freedom, creativity, and joy without feeling overwhelmed or out of control. Peace in this chakra involves emotional fluidity and the ability to go with the flow of life without excessive attachment or resistance.

Emotional Balance: The Sacral Chakra helps regulate emotions, preventing them from becoming overwhelming. When balanced, it fosters emotional resilience, allowing you to experience emotions without being consumed by them.

Pleasure and Joy: When the Sacral Chakra is open, you embrace the pleasures of life and allow yourself to enjoy the present moment, leading to a sense of peace.

Letting Go of Guilt: Many emotional blocks come from guilt or shame. The Sacral Chakra helps release these limiting emotions and encourages self-acceptance.

Affirmations: "I allow my emotions to flow freely without judgment."

Creative Expression: Engage in artistic activities, dance, or anything that helps you connect to your emotional world in a creative way.

Crystals: Carnelian, Moonstone, and Orange Calcite help balance emotions and promote creativity and joy.

3. Solar Plexus Chakra (Manipura) and Peace

The Solar Plexus Chakra is the center of personal power, will, and self-esteem. A balanced Solar Plexus Chakra brings peace by fostering confidence, self-worth, and a sense of inner strength. When you are connected to your personal power, you are less likely to be shaken by external circumstances or the opinions of others.

Confidence and Self-Worth: Inner peace often comes from the belief that you are worthy and capable. The Solar Plexus Chakra empowers you to trust your abilities and navigate life with confidence.

Self-Control: This chakra governs our ability to control our impulses and reactions. A balanced Solar Plexus Chakra allows you to maintain composure and make decisions calmly.

Emotional Independence: With a healthy Solar Plexus, you are not easily influenced by others' opinions or the outside world. This independence leads to inner peace because you are not reliant on external validation.

Affirmations: "I am in peace with myself."

Meditation and Visualization: Visualize yourself as a strong, calm and, confident individual who is unaffected by negativity.

Crystals: Citrine, Yellow Jasper, and Tiger's Eye help build confidence, personal power, and self-respect.

4. Heart Chakra (Anahata) and Peace

The Heart Chakra is the center of love, compassion, and forgiveness. It is directly connected to inner peace, as love and compassion are the most potent antidotes to fear, anger, and resentment. When the Heart Chakra is balanced, we feel connected to others, and our relationships are harmonious, fostering peace both internally and externally.

Unconditional Love: The Heart Chakra invites unconditional love, not just for others but for oneself. Love is the foundation of peace, as it dissolves conflict and fosters harmony.

Forgiveness: A blocked Heart Chakra can harbor grudges and resentment. Balancing this chakra encourages forgiveness, which is essential for peace. Forgiveness frees you from emotional pain and negativity.

Compassion for All: The Heart Chakra fosters empathy and compassion, helping you understand others' perspectives and creating peaceful relationships.

Affirmations: "I am at peace with myself and others."

Acts of Kindness: Practice random acts of kindness or volunteer. This not only opens the Heart Chakra but also creates a sense of inner peace through connection.

Crystals: Rose Quartz, Green Aventurine, and Malachite are excellent for healing emotional wounds and fostering love and peace.

5. Throat Chakra (Vishuddha) and Peace

The Throat Chakra governs communication and self-expression. Peace is achieved through clear, honest, and compassionate communication. When the Throat Chakra is balanced, we can express ourselves authentically, speak our truth, and communicate with others peacefully.

Honest Communication: Peace begins with clear and honest communication. A balanced Throat Chakra ensures that you express your thoughts and feelings with clarity and compassion.

Speaking Your Truth: When you are in touch with your true self and can communicate that truth to others, you experience a sense of inner peace because you are no longer hiding or suppressing your voice.

Listening with Compassion: Peaceful communication also involves listening. The Throat Chakra helps you listen attentively and with empathy, which fosters mutual understanding and harmony.

Affirmations: "I speak and listen to truth."

Journaling or Writing: Express your feelings and thoughts through writing, which helps open the Throat Chakra and clear emotional blocks.

Crystals: Lapis Lazuli, Aquamarine, and Turquoise support honest communication and self-expression.

6. Third Eye Chakra (Ajna) and Peace

The Third Eye Chakra is the center of intuition, wisdom, and perception. Peace arises when we can see beyond the surface of things and understand the deeper truths of life. The Third Eye Chakra enables clarity, mental calmness, and the ability to navigate life with wisdom and insight.

Clarity and Insight: The Third Eye Chakra helps you gain clarity in situations, enabling you to make decisions that align with your higher self. This clarity fosters peace because it eliminates confusion and doubt.

Intuition: Trusting your intuition helps you navigate life peacefully. When you listen to your inner wisdom, you make choices that are aligned with your true path, reducing conflict and stress.

Perspective: A balanced Third Eye Chakra helps you see situations from a broader perspective, helping you approach life with patience and acceptance.

Affirmations: "I see clearly and make decisions that bring me peace."

Meditation: Practice meditation focused on opening your Third Eye. Visualizations that involve seeing yourself in a state of calm or clarity can also help.

Crystals: Amethyst, Fluorite, and Sodalite support clarity, intuition, and mental calm.

7. Crown Chakra (Sahasrara) and Peace

The Crown Chakra is the center of spiritual connection and enlightenment. It connects you to universal consciousness and helps you experience a deep sense of peace that transcends the material world. When the Crown Chakra is balanced, you feel connected to the divine and feel peace with the flow of life.

Spiritual Connection: The Crown Chakra helps you experience a sense of oneness with the universe. This spiritual connection fosters a deep, abiding peace that comes from knowing you are part of something greater than yourself.

Acceptance of Divine Will: When the Crown Chakra is open, you trust in the divine timing of life. This trust allows you to accept life as it comes, knowing that everything is unfolding for your highest good.

Letting Go of Attachments: The Crown Chakra helps you release attachments to material things, allowing you to find peace in the present moment.

Affirmations: "I find peace in the present moment."

Meditation: Focus on connecting with the divine or universal energy. Practice surrendering to the greater flow of life.

Crystals: Clear Quartz, Amethyst, and Selenite help connect to the higher realms and foster spiritual peace.

CHAPTER XXIII

CHAKRAS AND FEARS

Exploring the relationship between chakras and fears reveals how deeply intertwined our emotional, physical, and spiritual health is with our inner energy system. Each chakra governs a specific area of life, and fears related to each chakra can cause blockages or imbalances in the flow of energy, leading to physical and emotional issues.

By working with each chakra to address the specific fears related to it, you can release blockages and restore harmony within your body and mind.

1. Root Chakra (Muladhara) – Fear of Survival, Security, and Stability

Fear: Fear of survival, financial insecurity, fear of being unsupported, fear of change, or fear of being abandoned.

Impact: This fear is deeply connected to basic needs like food, shelter, and safety. If the root chakra is imbalanced or blocked, it can manifest in feelings of anxiety, worry about money or safety, chronic fatigue, and even physical issues like lower back pain or digestive problems.

Addressing the Fear: Grounding exercises, connecting with nature, affirmations of safety and stability, and engaging in physical activities can help balance this chakra.

2. Sacral Chakra (Svadhisthana) – Fear of Emotions, Sexuality, and Creativity

Fear: Fear of emotional vulnerability, fear of intimacy or rejection, fear of being controlled or not being able to express desires, fear of rejection in relationships, or fear of one's own creative potential.

Impact: An imbalance in the sacral chakra can manifest as emotional numbness, creative blocks, lack of sexual desire, or difficulty in forming healthy relationships. It can also lead to emotional instability, such as intense mood swings or depression.

Addressing the Fear: Engaging in creative activities, practicing healthy emotional expression, exploring sensuality in a safe and nurturing way, and working on self-worth can help heal this chakra.

3. Solar Plexus Chakra (Manipura) – Fear of Power, Control, and Self-Worth

Fear: Fear of failure, fear of not being good enough, fear of criticism or rejection, fear of being powerless, fear of making decisions, or fear of not being in control of one's life.

Impact: This fear is tied to self-esteem, confidence, and personal power. A blocked or weakened solar plexus chakra can cause indecisiveness, low self-worth, poor digestion, and a sense of being disconnected from one's personal power.

Addressing the Fear: Building self-confidence, practicing assertiveness, engaging in physical exercises that strengthen the core (like yoga), and setting small achievable goals can help heal and empower the solar plexus chakra.

4. Heart Chakra (Anahata) – Fear of Love, Rejection, and Emotional Vulnerability

Fear: Fear of being hurt or betrayed in relationships, fear of opening up emotionally, fear of not being loved or accepted, or fear of being abandoned.

Impact: The heart chakra governs love, compassion, and emotional balance. When blocked, it can lead to emotional isolation, difficulty forming deep connections, feelings of loneliness, or physical ailments like chest pain, heart problems, or respiratory issues.

Addressing the Fear: Practicing forgiveness (towards yourself and others), engaging in acts of self-love, being vulnerable in healthy relationships, and working through past trauma can help heal the heart chakra.

5. Throat Chakra (Vishuddha) – Fear of Expression and Communication

Fear: Fear of speaking one's truth, fear of being misunderstood or judged, fear of not being heard, or fear of speaking up in general.

Impact: Fear related to the throat chakra can lead to difficulty communicating effectively, fear of public speaking, or feeling stifled in relationships. It can also manifest in physical symptoms like sore throats, neck stiffness, or thyroid issues.

Addressing the Fear: Practicing clear and honest communication, expressing yourself through writing or speaking, engaging in vocal exercises, and using affirmations for self-expression can help balance the throat chakra.

6. Third Eye Chakra (Ajna) – Fear of Intuition, Perception, and the Unknown

Fear: Fear of trusting intuition, fear of the unknown, fear of not seeing things clearly, or fear of being spiritually "blind." It can also relate to the fear of not understanding your life's purpose.

Impact: When the third eye chakra is blocked or imbalanced, it can lead to confusion, lack of clarity, indecisiveness, or difficulty trusting your instincts. You may also experience headaches, vision problems, or mental fog.

Addressing the Fear: Engaging in meditation, practicing mindfulness, trusting your gut feelings, and developing a connection to your inner wisdom can help heal the third eye chakra.

7. Crown Chakra (Sahasrara) – Fear of Spiritual Disconnection, Meaninglessness

Fear: Fear of spiritual emptiness, fear of losing connection with the divine, fear of death or the afterlife, or fear of not having a higher purpose in life.

Impact: A blocked or unbalanced crown chakra can result in feelings of spiritual confusion, a lack of purpose, mental exhaustion, or feeling disconnected from a greater meaning in life. It can also lead to depression or existential crises.

Addressing the Fear: Engaging in spiritual practices (such as prayer, meditation, or mindfulness), seeking connection with a higher power, exploring your life's purpose, and embracing spiritual growth can help open and heal the crown chakra.

CHAPTER XXIV

CHAKRAS AND LOW ENERGY

A lack of energy often has a profound connection to imbalances in the chakras, the body's energy centers. Each chakra plays a role in how energy flows through your physical, emotional, and spiritual systems. When one or more chakras are blocked or underactive, it can result in fatigue, lethargy, or a sense of being "stuck." Here's a deep dive into how each chakra relates to energy levels, why imbalances happen, and how to restore vitality.

1. Root Chakra (Muladhara): Energy Foundation

Connection to Energy: The root chakra anchors you to Earth's energy, providing a sense of stability and physical vitality. A blocked root chakra leads to feelings of insecurity and physical exhaustion.

Signs of Imbalance:

Chronic fatigue or weakness

Anxiety and restlessness

Financial or physical instability

Causes:

Unresolved survival fears (money, shelter, health)

Disconnection from nature or physical activity

Restoration Practices:

Grounding exercises like walking barefoot on soil

Eating root vegetables (carrots, potatoes)

Affirmation: "I am grounded, safe, and supported."

2. Sacral Chakra (Svadhisthana): Emotional Energy

Connection to Energy: This chakra governs emotional energy, creativity, and pleasure. An imbalance can cause emotional exhaustion or apathy.

Signs of Imbalance:

Lack of enthusiasm or joy

Feeling uninspired or "numb"

Reproductive or lower abdominal issues

Causes:

Repressed emotions or creativity

Guilt or shame from past actions

Restoration Practices:

Water therapy: baths, swimming, or visualizing flowing water

Creative activities like painting or dancing

Affirmation: "I embrace my emotions and creativity freely."

3. Solar Plexus Chakra (Manipura): Personal Power

Connection to Energy: The solar plexus fuels physical energy and willpower. When blocked, it results in low motivation and a sense of powerlessness.

Signs of Imbalance:

Procrastination or lack of direction

Digestive issues

Overwhelm or burnout from overexertion

Causes:

Self-doubt or fear of failure

Overworking without rest

Restoration Practices:

Sunlight exposure (solar energy)

Breath of fire (rapid kapalbathi breathing technique)

Affirmation: "I am confident, strong, and full of energy."

4. Heart Chakra (Anahata): Emotional Vitality

Connection to Energy: The heart chakra fuels emotional resilience and compassion. Blockages here lead to emotional fatigue or feelings of isolation.

Signs of Imbalance:

Lack of empathy or connection with others

Physical fatigue, especially in the chest or upper body

Holding onto grudges or past heartbreaks

Causes:

Unforgiveness or unresolved grief

Isolation or lack of self-love

Restoration Practices:

Loving-kindness meditation (Metta)

Heart-opening yoga poses (Camel Pose, Cobra Pose)

Affirmation: "I am open to giving and receiving love."

5. Throat Chakra (Vishuddha): Expressive Energy

Connection to Energy: Governs the energy of communication and expression. Blockages can create mental fatigue and resistance to sharing thoughts.

Signs of Imbalance:

Feeling unheard or unable to express yourself

Chronic throat issues or stiffness in the neck

Mental exhaustion from overthinking

Causes:

Suppressed thoughts or truths

Fear of judgment

Restoration Practices:

Vocal toning or chanting "Ham"

Journaling your thoughts freely

Affirmation: "I express myself with clarity and confidence."

6. Third Eye Chakra (Ajna): Mental Energy

Connection to Energy: Governs mental clarity, intuition, and focus. A blocked third eye leads to brain fog, confusion, and a lack of inspiration.

Signs of Imbalance:

Overthinking or indecisiveness

Headaches or vision problems

Feeling disconnected from intuition

Causes:

Information overload

Ignoring intuitive insights

Restoration Practices:

Visualization exercises (imagine an indigo light at your forehead)

Meditation to calm the mind

Affirmation: "I trust my intuition and inner wisdom."

7. Crown Chakra (Sahasrara): Spiritual Energy

Connection to Energy: Represents your connection to universal energy. Blockages result in spiritual fatigue or feeling "cut off" from purpose.

Signs of Imbalance:

Feeling lost or purposeless

Sleep disturbances

Migraines or pressure in the head

Causes:

Attachment to material concerns

Resistance to spiritual growth

Restoration Practices:

Silence meditation or prayer

Spending time in nature to connect with universal energy

Affirmation: “I am connected to divine energy.”

CHAPTER XXV

CHAKRAS AND PROCRASTINATION

Procrastination often stems from imbalances in one or more chakras, as these energy centers govern motivation, focus, self-discipline, and emotional resilience. By understanding the energetic roots of procrastination and addressing them, you can shift from stagnation to action.

1. Root Chakra (Muladhara): Procrastination from Fear and Instability

Energetic Link to Procrastination: A blocked root chakra manifests as a lack of grounding, creating fear and insecurity about taking action. Fear of failure or financial instability often keeps people stuck in analysis paralysis.

Signs of Root Chakra Procrastination:

Avoiding tasks because they feel overwhelming or "unsafe."

Feeling unmotivated due to general fatigue or disconnection from basic needs.

Healing Techniques:

Grounding Practices: Spend time in nature, practice grounding yoga poses like Mountain Pose, or visualize roots anchoring you to the Earth.

Affirmations: "I am secure and capable of taking action."

Crystals: Meditate with red jasper or smoky quartz for grounding.

2. Sacral Chakra (Svadhisthana): Procrastination from Emotional Resistance

Energetic Link to Procrastination: Emotional discomfort or fear of imperfection can arise from an imbalanced sacral chakra, leading to avoidance of creative or emotionally charged tasks.

Signs of Sacral Chakra Procrastination:

Putting off creative work due to a lack of inspiration or fear of judgment.

Avoiding tasks involving emotional vulnerability (e.g., difficult conversations).

Healing Techniques:

Creative Flow Activities: Engage in low-pressure creative exercises like sketching or freewriting to reignite enthusiasm.

Water Rituals: Use water (baths, swimming) to cleanse emotional stagnation.

Affirmations: "I embrace creativity and joy in all I do."

3. Solar Plexus Chakra (Manipura): Procrastination from Low Confidence

Energetic Link to Procrastination: The solar plexus governs willpower, confidence, and self-discipline. A blocked or weak chakra here often results in self-doubt, leading to procrastination born from fear of failure or criticism.

Signs of Solar Plexus Chakra Procrastination:

Feeling paralyzed by perfectionism.

Difficulty starting tasks due to a lack of focus or drive.

Healing Techniques:

Fire Meditations: Visualize a golden flame in your solar plexus, fueling confidence and determination.

Small Wins: Break tasks into smaller steps and celebrate progress to rebuild willpower.

Affirmations: "I take bold, confident steps forward."

4. Heart Chakra (Anahata): Procrastination from Lack of Connection

Energetic Link to Procrastination: A blocked heart chakra can create feelings of disconnection or apathy toward tasks that involve helping others or working collaboratively.

Signs of Heart Chakra Procrastination:

Avoiding tasks that require emotional involvement or teamwork.

Feeling indifferent or unmotivated about your goals.

Healing Techniques:

Gratitude Practice: Reflect on the value of your work and how it contributes to others' well-being.

Heart-Opening Yoga: Try poses like Camel Pose or Bridge Pose to release stagnation in the chest.

Affirmations: "I approach my tasks with love and compassion."

5. Throat Chakra (Vishuddha): Procrastination from Fear of Expression

Energetic Link to Procrastination: A blocked throat chakra can result in hesitation to communicate or express ideas, leading to delays in work requiring communication or public presentation.

Signs of Throat Chakra Procrastination:

Putting off writing, speaking, or presenting tasks.

Overthinking or avoiding tasks due to fear of being misunderstood.

Healing Techniques:

Vocal Practices: Chant “Ham” or engage in humming exercises to stimulate your throat chakra.

Affirmations: "I express my thoughts clearly and confidently."

Crystals: Use aquamarine or blue lace agate to enhance communication.

6. Third Eye Chakra (Ajna): Procrastination from Lack of Clarity

Energetic Link to Procrastination: The third eye governs intuition and mental focus. A blocked third eye can create confusion or overwhelm, leading to delays in decision-making or planning.

Signs of Third Eye Chakra Procrastination:

Feeling stuck because of overthinking or inability to prioritize tasks.

Difficulty visualizing the outcomes of your efforts.

Healing Techniques:

Mindfulness Practices: Practice focused breathing or meditation to calm mental chatter.

Visualization Exercises: Imagine completing the task successfully to build motivation.

Affirmations: "I trust my intuition to guide my actions."

7. Crown Chakra (Sahasrara): Procrastination from Disconnection

Energetic Link to Procrastination: The crown chakra represents your connection to higher purpose and divine inspiration. A blocked crown chakra can result in procrastination from feeling aimless or spiritually disconnected.

Signs of Crown Chakra Procrastination:

Feeling unmotivated due to lack of meaning in your work.

Avoiding tasks because they feel mundane or disconnected from your purpose.

Healing Techniques:

Silence Meditation: Spend time in stillness to reconnect with your higher self.

Nature Therapy: Engage in activities that inspire awe, such as stargazing or hiking.

Affirmations: "I am aligned with my purpose."

CHAPTER XXVI

CHAKRAS AND OVER THINKING

Overthinking and overanalysis often result from imbalances in specific chakras, particularly those associated with mental clarity, intuition, and grounding. When energy flows unevenly in these areas, it can create mental loops that make it hard to move from thought to action.

1. Root Chakra (Muladhara): Lack of Grounding

Energetic Connection: The root chakra is your foundation. When underactive, it can make you feel ungrounded, leading to mental spirals as your mind searches for stability.

Overthinking Symptoms:

Worrying excessively about survival, safety, or material needs.

Feeling scattered and disconnected from the present.

Healing Techniques:

Grounding Exercises: Walk barefoot on grass or soil to reconnect with the Earth.

Breathing Techniques: Practice deep belly breathing to calm the nervous system.

Affirmation: "I am grounded and secure in my thoughts and actions."

2. Sacral Chakra (Svadhisthana): Emotional Overload

Energetic Connection: The sacral chakra governs emotions and creativity. An imbalance here can amplify emotional overanalysis, especially in relationships.

Overthinking Symptoms:

Replaying past emotional events or obsessing over interpersonal dynamics.

Difficulty distinguishing between intuition and emotional bias.

Healing Techniques:

Creative Flow Activities: Engage in painting, writing, or dancing to redirect emotional energy.

Water Rituals: Take a warm bath or visualize water cleansing emotional clutter.

Affirmation: "I trust the flow of my emotions and let them guide me gently."

3. Solar Plexus Chakra (Manipura): Self-Doubt and Mental Paralysis

Energetic Connection: The solar plexus governs personal power and decision-making. An underactive or overactive solar plexus can lead to excessive self-doubt or overanalysis of choices.

Overthinking Symptoms:

Overanalyzing decisions due to fear of making the wrong choice.

Struggling with perfectionism or fear of criticism.

Healing Techniques:

Sunlight Meditation: Visualize the warmth of the sun strengthening your confidence.

Small Decisions Practice: Make small, quick decisions to train decisiveness.

Affirmation: "I trust my judgment and make decisions with ease."

4. Heart Chakra (Anahata): Overthinking Relationships

Energetic Connection: The heart chakra governs compassion, love, and forgiveness. Overanalysis often occurs when this chakra is blocked, especially in matters of the heart.

Overthinking Symptoms:

Ruminating about unresolved relationship issues.

Excessively worrying about being understood or accepted.

Healing Techniques:

Heart-Opening Yoga: Practice poses like Camel Pose or Bridge Pose.

Gratitude Journaling: Focus on the positive aspects of your relationships.

Affirmation: "I trust in the love and harmony within my relationships."

5. Throat Chakra (Vishuddha): Mental Chatter and Unexpressed Thoughts

Energetic Connection: The throat chakra governs communication and self-expression. Blockages here can lead to internal mental chatter and unexpressed ideas spinning in your head.

Overthinking Symptoms:

Mentally rehearsing conversations or replaying past ones.

Struggling to articulate thoughts clearly.

Healing Techniques:

Vocal Release: Chant, sing, or hum to clear pent-up energy.

Write It Out: Journaling helps articulate and release thoughts.

Affirmation: "I communicate my thoughts and ideas with clarity."

6. Third Eye Chakra (Ajna): Mental Overload and Lack of Clarity

Energetic Connection: The third eye chakra governs intuition, imagination, and mental clarity. An overactive third eye can lead to obsessive thinking, while a blocked one causes confusion.

Overthinking Symptoms:

Difficulty trusting intuition, leading to constant questioning.

Feeling overwhelmed by conflicting thoughts or too much information.

Healing Techniques:

Visualization Practices: Focus on an indigo light at your forehead, calming mental energy.

Screen Detox: Limit screen time to reduce overstimulation.

Affirmation: "I trust my intuition and see clearly through mental fog."

7. Crown Chakra (Sahasrara): Overanalysis from Disconnection

Energetic Connection: The crown chakra governs your connection to higher consciousness and universal wisdom. Overthinking often arises when disconnected from your sense of purpose or divine guidance.

Overthinking Symptoms:

Feeling stuck in the “how” rather than trusting the flow of life.

Obsessing over existential or spiritual questions without resolution.

Healing Techniques:

Meditation on Stillness: Sit in quiet reflection, letting thoughts pass like clouds.

Connection Practices: Spend time in nature or practice prayer to reconnect spiritually.

Affirmation: "I am aligned with the divine flow of life."

CHAPTER XXVII

CHAKRAS AND LYING

Lying, whether to oneself or others, can stem from specific imbalances or overactivity in certain chakras. The act of lying disrupts the natural energy flow, creating blockages or distortions that affect your emotional, mental, and spiritual well-being. Below is an in-depth exploration of the connection between chakras and lying, including the energetic causes and healing techniques.

Here the order of chakras are re-arranged in descending order of imbalance in relation to lying.

1. Throat Chakra (Vishuddha): The Core of Truth and ExpressionEnergetic Role:

The throat chakra governs communication, truth-telling, and self-expression. When balanced, it fosters honest, clear, and authentic speech.

Connection to Lying: A blocked or overactive throat chakra often leads to lying due to fear of judgment, inability to express oneself honestly, or manipulation.

Signs of Imbalance Related to Lying:

Chronic throat issues, such as a sore throat or tightness.

Feeling unable to express thoughts or overcompensating with exaggeration.

Guilt or anxiety after lying.

Healing Techniques:

Chanting or Singing: Use the mantra "Ham" to activate the throat chakra.

Authenticity Practices: Start journaling about your thoughts and feelings to cultivate honesty.

Affirmation: "I speak my truth with clarity and integrity."

2. Solar Plexus Chakra (Manipura): Confidence in TruthEnergetic Role:

This chakra governs self-esteem, personal power, and the courage to stand by your values.

Connection to Lying:

Lying often arises from a lack of confidence in the truth or fear of how it will be received.

A weakened solar plexus might lead to lying as a form of self-protection or avoiding conflict.

Signs of Imbalance Related to Lying:

Avoiding responsibility or accountability.

Overly controlling behavior to maintain false perceptions.

Healing Techniques:

Self-Empowerment Exercises: Reflect on situations where honesty brought positive outcomes.

Sunlight Exposure: Spend time in the sun to energize this chakra.

Affirmation: "I stand confidently in my truth."

3. Sacral Chakra (Svadhisthana): Emotional HonestyEnergetic Role:

This chakra governs emotions, relationships, and creativity. A balanced sacral chakra allows you to express emotions honestly without fear of rejection.

Connection to Lying:

Emotional dishonesty, such as lying about feelings or desires, often stems from sacral chakra imbalances.

Lies in intimate relationships frequently indicate blocked energy here.

Signs of Imbalance Related to Lying:

Suppressing or distorting emotions.

Difficulty being vulnerable or authentic in relationships.

Healing Techniques:

Emotional Awareness: Practice identifying and naming your emotions.

Water Therapy: Use baths or swimming to release pent-up energy.

Affirmation: "I honor my emotions and express them truthfully."

4. Heart Chakra (Anahata): Integrity in RelationshipsEnergetic Role:

The heart chakra fosters empathy, compassion, and genuine connection. Lying disrupts the energy of trust and love.

Connection to Lying:

Lies told to protect oneself or others can stem from a wounded heart chakra. This may include white lies, people-pleasing, or fear of rejection.

Signs of Imbalance Related to Lying:

Difficulty forgiving oneself or others for dishonesty.

Feeling disconnected or guilty after lying.

Healing Techniques:

Loving-Kindness Meditation: Focus on forgiving yourself and others for dishonesty.

Heart-Opening Yoga Poses: Camel Pose, Bridge Pose, or Cobra Pose.

Affirmation: "I live in harmony with myself and others."

5. Third Eye Chakra (Ajna): Clarity and Awareness of TruthEnergetic Role:

The third eye chakra governs intuition, insight, and perception of truth. Lying, particularly to oneself, is linked to a distorted third eye.

Connection to Lying:

Self-deception and denial are hallmarks of third-eye imbalances.

Lies driven by confusion or lack of clarity often originate here.

Signs of Imbalance Related to Lying:

Overthinking and rationalizing dishonesty.

Feeling disconnected from inner truth or intuition.

Healing Techniques:

Meditation on Insight: Visualize a bright indigo light at your forehead, clearing illusions.

Decisiveness Practice: Commit to small truthful decisions daily to strengthen trust in your intuition.

Affirmation: "I see and accept truth with clarity."

6. Root Chakra (Muladhara): Lying as a Survival MechanismEnergetic Role:

The root chakra governs survival instincts and security. Lying to protect yourself or gain stability often originates from imbalances here.

Connection to Lying:

Lies motivated by fear of losing resources, status, or safety can indicate a blocked root chakra.

Signs of Imbalance Related to Lying:

Anxiety or fear-driven dishonesty.

Overemphasis on material stability at the expense of truth.

Healing Techniques:

Grounding Exercises: Walk barefoot on natural ground to stabilize energy.

Red Foods: Eat foods like beets and strawberries to energize the root chakra.

Affirmation: "I am safe and secure in my truth."

CHAPTER XXVIII

CHAKRAS AND OVER CONFIDENCE

Overconfidence, while seemingly a positive trait, can arise from imbalances or overactivity in certain chakras, particularly those associated with personal power, expression, and intuition. When these energy centers are out of balance, overconfidence can manifest as arrogance, dismissiveness, or a lack of self-awareness.

Here the order of chakras are re-arranged in descending order of imbalance in relation to over-confidence.

1. Solar Plexus Chakra (Manipura): The Core of Personal Power

Energetic Role: The solar plexus chakra governs self-esteem, willpower, and personal power. When overactive, it can lead to an inflated sense of self and overconfidence.

Signs of Overactivity:

Dominating conversations or situations without considering others.

Overestimating abilities, leading to overpromising or taking unnecessary risks.

Dismissing constructive criticism or feedback.

Healing Techniques:

Humility Practices: Reflect on moments when collaboration or learning from others benefited you.

Fire Element Balance: While the solar plexus is associated with fire, excessive energy here needs cooling practices like swimming or visualizing a calm blue light.

Affirmation: "I lead with confidence, humility, and respect for others."

2. Throat Chakra (Vishuddha): Overexpression of Ideas

Energetic Role: The throat chakra governs communication and self-expression. An overactive throat chakra can result in speaking excessively or forcefully to assert dominance or authority.

Signs of Overactivity:

Interrupting others or dominating conversations.

Being overly assertive or dismissive of others' viewpoints.

Overpromising due to overconfidence in communication skills.

Healing Techniques:

Listening Practices: Dedicate time to active listening without interjecting.

Blue Light Meditation: Visualize a soothing blue light at your throat, calming and balancing its energy.

Affirmation: "I express myself thoughtfully and listen with care."

3. Third Eye Chakra (Ajna): Overconfidence in Intuition

Energetic Role: The third eye governs intuition, perception, and insight. Overactivity can result in overestimating one's intuition, leading to impulsive decisions without rational consideration.

Signs of Overactivity:

Acting impulsively based on "gut feelings" without assessing facts.

Believing one's perspective is always correct or superior.

Overanalyzing others' actions while failing to reflect on oneself.

Healing Techniques:

Critical Thinking Practices: Balance intuition with rational analysis by fact-checking or seeking advice.

Indigo Visualization: Focus on an indigo light calming the third eye to bring clarity and humility.

Affirmation: "I trust my intuition while staying open to other perspectives."

4. Heart Chakra (Anahata): Overconfidence in Relationships

Energetic Role: The heart chakra governs love, compassion, and connection. Overconfidence can manifest as believing one's emotional approach is always correct, leading to controlling or dismissive behavior.

Signs of Overactivity:

Offering unsolicited advice or assuming you know what's best for others.

Being overly generous with expectations of recognition or reciprocation.

Focusing on "fixing" others rather than fostering mutual growth.

Healing Techniques:

Empathy Practices: Actively seek to understand others' perspectives without offering solutions.

Green Light Meditation: Visualize a soft green light radiating from your heart, fostering humility and compassion.

Affirmation: "I nurture relationships with humility and respect."

5. Crown Chakra (Sahasrara): Spiritual Ego and Overconfidence

Energetic Role: The crown chakra governs spiritual connection and universal understanding. Overconfidence here can lead to a "spiritual ego," where one believes they are more enlightened or superior to others.

Signs of Overactivity:

Feeling "above" others in terms of spirituality or intellect.

Using spiritual knowledge as a means to assert dominance.

Dismissing others' spiritual paths as inferior.

Healing Techniques:

Humility Meditation: Reflect on the interconnectedness of all beings and the infinite nature of growth and learning.

Gratitude Practices: Regularly express gratitude for the wisdom and support you receive from others.

Affirmation: "I am a vessel of wisdom and remain humble in my journey."

6. Root Chakra (Muladhara): Overconfidence in Stability

Energetic Role: The root chakra governs grounding and survival. Overconfidence here can manifest as taking stability, safety, or resources for granted.

Signs of Overactivity:

Overestimating your ability to handle challenges without preparation.

Ignoring foundational needs, like financial planning or physical health, due to excessive trust in stability.

Healing Techniques:

Grounding Practices: Engage in activities like gardening, hiking, or mindful walking to reconnect with reality.

Red Light Visualization: Balance the root chakra by visualizing a steady, glowing red light at the base of your spine.

Affirmation: "I honor and nurture my foundations with care."

7. Sacral Chakra (Svadhisthana): Overconfidence in Emotions

Energetic Role: The sacral chakra governs emotions and relationships. Overconfidence here can manifest as being overly assertive in expressing emotions or assuming emotional control over others.

Signs of Overactivity:

Overasserting your emotions as more valid or important than others'.

Using charm or manipulation to dominate relationships.

Healing Techniques:

Emotional Reflection: Practice pausing before reacting emotionally to assess balance.

Water Rituals: Spend time near water to soothe emotional overactivity.

Affirmation: "I honor the emotions of others as equal to my own."

CHAPTER XXIX

CHAKRAS AND RELATIONSHIP

Chakras play a significant role in how we experience relationships, both with ourselves and with others. Each chakra governs different aspects of emotional, physical, and spiritual energy that directly influence how we connect, communicate, and relate to those around us. By understanding the connection between the chakras and relationships, we can better navigate and heal our interactions with others.

1. Root Chakra and Relationships

Focus: Safety, Security, and Trust

The Root Chakra (Muladhara) governs your sense of safety, security, and grounding. When this chakra is balanced, it fosters trust, stability, and the ability to build secure, healthy relationships.

Impact on Relationships: A balanced Root Chakra helps you feel safe in relationships, whether romantic, familial, or friendships. It allows you to trust others and feel comfortable in your environment.

Imbalance Symptoms: If the Root Chakra is blocked or imbalanced, you may feel insecure, anxious, or fearful in relationships. You may struggle with trust issues, dependency, or difficulty committing.

Healing and Balance:

Grounding Practices: Spend time in nature, walk barefoot, or practice grounding exercises to feel more secure.

Self-Affirmation: Repeat affirmations like, "I am safe, secure, and supported in my relationships."

Root Chakra Healing: Using red stones like Garnet or Bloodstone, and essential oils like Vetiver or Cedarwood, can help enhance stability and trust in your relationships.

2. Sacral Chakra and Relationships

Focus: Creativity, Sexuality, and Emotional Expression

The Sacral Chakra (Svadhisthana) governs creativity, emotional expression, and sexuality. It is the center of desire, pleasure, and intimacy.

Impact on Relationships: A healthy Sacral Chakra helps you experience healthy emotional connections, intimacy, and creative expression in relationships. It fosters mutual respect for each other's boundaries and a deeper emotional connection.

Imbalance Symptoms: An imbalanced Sacral Chakra can manifest as difficulty expressing emotions, sexual dysfunction, or fear of intimacy. You may feel emotionally distant or struggle with codependency.

Healing and Balance:

Emotional Expression: Practice expressing your emotions openly and creatively, whether through art, journaling, or other forms of self-expression.

Sexual Healing: If there are sexual challenges, work on self-love and self-acceptance to improve intimacy.

Sacral Chakra Healing: Use Carnelian or Orange Calcite crystals, and essential oils like Ylang Ylang or Jasmine to stimulate passion, creativity, and emotional healing.

3. Solar Plexus Chakra and Relationships

Focus: Personal Power, Confidence, and Boundaries

The Solar Plexus Chakra (Manipura) is the center of personal power, self-esteem, and confidence. It governs your ability to assert yourself in relationships and maintain healthy boundaries.

Impact on Relationships: A balanced Solar Plexus Chakra helps you set clear boundaries, feel confident in your relationships, and communicate your needs assertively without being overly dominant or passive.

Imbalance Symptoms: If the Solar Plexus is out of balance, you may struggle with low self-esteem, difficulty asserting yourself, or being overly controlling. You might also struggle with feeling powerless or lacking confidence in your relationship.

Healing and Balance:

Self-Empowerment: Practice affirmations like, "I trust my power, and I set healthy boundaries in my relationships."

Confidence Building: Engage in activities that boost your self-esteem, such as exercise or accomplishing small personal goals.

Solar Plexus Healing: Use crystals like Citrine or Tiger's Eye, and essential oils like Lemon or Peppermint to promote confidence and self-assurance in relationships.

4. Heart Chakra and Relationships

Focus: Love, Compassion, and Forgiveness

The Heart Chakra (Anahata) is the center of love, compassion, and emotional healing. It governs the ability to give and receive love in healthy, balanced ways.

Impact on Relationships: When the Heart Chakra is open and balanced, you can give and receive love freely, creating harmonious and loving connections with others. It enhances empathy, compassion, and emotional intimacy in all relationships.

Imbalance Symptoms: If the Heart Chakra is blocked or unbalanced, you may feel emotionally distant, have difficulty trusting others, or struggle with feelings of loneliness. There may also be difficulty in forgiving or opening up to love.

Healing and Balance:

Forgiveness: Practice forgiving yourself and others to release emotional blockages and open your heart to love.

Compassionate Listening: Engage in active listening and empathic communication to deepen emotional connection in relationships.

Heart Chakra Healing: Use Rose Quartz or Green Aventurine crystals, and essential oils like Rose or Geranium to promote love, healing, and compassion.

5. Throat Chakra and Relationships

Focus: Communication, Truth, and Expression

The Throat Chakra (Vishuddha) governs communication, both in terms of speaking your truth and listening to others. It's the center of verbal and non-verbal expression.

Impact on Relationships: A balanced Throat Chakra facilitates open, honest communication in relationships. You can express yourself clearly and listen attentively, fostering deeper understanding and connection.

Imbalance Symptoms: An imbalanced Throat Chakra may cause you to have difficulty speaking up for yourself, fear of speaking your truth, or an inability to express yourself fully. You may also feel misunderstood or have issues with gossip or dishonesty.

Healing and Balance:

Honest Communication: Practice expressing your thoughts and feelings openly, even if it's uncomfortable.

Active Listening: Foster healthy communication by listening attentively without judgment or interruption.

Throat Chakra Healing: Use crystals like Aquamarine or Blue Lace Agate, and essential oils like Peppermint or Chamomile to support clear, authentic communication in your relationships.

6. Third Eye Chakra and Relationships

Focus: Intuition, Clarity, and Insight

The Third Eye Chakra (Ajna) governs intuition, inner wisdom, and the ability to see beyond surface-level dynamics in relationships.

Impact on Relationships: A balanced Third Eye Chakra allows you to intuitively understand others' feelings, recognize the deeper motivations in relationships, and have clarity in decision-making. It also helps you trust your instincts about people.

Imbalance Symptoms: If this chakra is blocked, you may feel confused, disconnected from your intuition, or struggle to understand your own or others' feelings. You may also be overly analytical or skeptical in your relationships.

Healing and Balance:

Trust Your Intuition: Practice listening to your inner voice when it comes to decisions and interactions in your relationships.

Meditation and Visualization: Spend time meditating to strengthen your connection to your inner wisdom and higher self.

Third Eye Chakra Healing: Use Amethyst or Lapis Lazuli crystals, and essential oils like Frankincense or Sandalwood to enhance intuition and gain clarity in relationships.

7. Crown Chakra and Relationships

Focus: Spiritual Connection, Higher Wisdom, and Universal Love

The Crown Chakra (Sahasrara) governs our connection to the divine, spiritual understanding, and the experience of unity with all beings.

Impact on Relationships: A balanced Crown Chakra helps you view relationships from a higher perspective, allowing you to see the divine spark in others and experience unconditional love. It fosters a sense of interconnectedness with all people.

Imbalance Symptoms: If the Crown Chakra is blocked, you may feel disconnected, isolated, or spiritually lost in relationships. You may also experience difficulty accepting others or feel a lack of purpose in your connections.

Healing and Balance:

Spiritual Connection: Practice mindfulness, meditation, or prayer to deepen your connection to the divine and the interconnectedness of all beings.

Non-Attachment: Practice detaching from the need to control relationships, allowing them to evolve naturally.

Crown Chakra Healing: Use Clear Quartz or Selenite crystals, and essential oils like Lavender or Neroli to support spiritual awakening and unity in relationships.

Tips for Chakra-Healing in Relationships:

1. Self-Awareness: Regularly assess the state of your chakras and how they may be affecting your relationships. When you're aware of potential imbalances, you can actively work on healing them.

2. Healthy Boundaries: Set clear boundaries to protect your energy and maintain balance in relationships, particularly when working on the Solar Plexus and Root Chakras.

3. Communication: Practice open, honest, and compassionate communication, especially for the Throat Chakra. This will help

you to express yourself clearly and listen effectively in your relationships.

4. Emotional Healing: Engage in practices that allow emotional release and healing, especially for the Heart and Sacral Chakras. This might include therapy, journaling, or energy healing.

5. Mutual Support: Encourage mutual growth and support in relationships, recognizing that healing each chakra contributes to collective well-being.

CHAPTER XXX

CHAKRAS AND COMMUNICATION

Effective communication is essential for building healthy relationships, and the chakras play a crucial role in how we express ourselves and listen to others. The Throat Chakra (Vishuddha) is the primary chakra involved in communication, but all of the chakras influence how we communicate and connect with others.

1. Root Chakra and Communication

Focus: Safety, Trust, and Grounding

The Root Chakra (Muladhara) is all about grounding, stability, and safety. It affects the foundation of how we express ourselves.

Impact on Communication: A balanced Root Chakra helps you feel secure and safe, allowing you to communicate openly without fear or hesitation. It builds the foundation for honest and authentic communication.

Imbalance Symptoms: If the Root Chakra is imbalanced, you may feel insecure or afraid to speak up. You may struggle with expressing your true feelings or may retreat into silence due to fear of rejection or instability.

Healing Practices:

Grounding Techniques: Practice grounding exercises like walking barefoot, spending time in nature, or sitting with your feet firmly on the ground to feel more secure in communication.

Affirmations: "I am safe and secure in expressing myself."

Root Chakra Stones: Use Hematite, Black Tourmaline, or Red Jasper to feel more stable and secure in your communication.

2. Sacral Chakra and Communication

Focus: Emotional Expression, Creativity, and Sensuality

The Sacral Chakra (Svadhisthana) governs emotions, creativity, and pleasure, and it influences how we communicate our feelings.

Impact on Communication: When the Sacral Chakra is balanced, you can express emotions freely, creating deep emotional connections with others. You're able to share your desires and needs in a healthy, creative way.

Imbalance Symptoms: If the Sacral Chakra is blocked, you may struggle with expressing your emotions, especially in vulnerable or intimate settings. You might have difficulty talking about your feelings, desires, or creativity.

Healing Practices:

Creative Expression: Engage in creative activities like painting, writing, or dancing to open up your emotional flow and enhance your ability to communicate your inner world.

Emotional Sharing: Practice being open with your feelings and allowing yourself to express joy, sadness, or desires without shame or guilt.

Sacral Chakra Stones: Use Carnelian, Orange Calcite, or Moonstone to enhance emotional expression and creativity in communication.

3. Solar Plexus Chakra and Communication

Focus: Personal Power, Confidence, and Assertiveness

The Solar Plexus Chakra (Manipura) is the center of confidence, personal power, and self-expression.

Impact on Communication: A balanced Solar Plexus Chakra helps you express yourself with clarity and confidence. You're able to communicate your thoughts and feelings assertively without being overly dominant or passive.

Imbalance Symptoms: If the Solar Plexus Chakra is imbalanced, you may find it difficult to speak up for yourself, or you may become overly controlling in your communication. You might also fear confrontation or struggle with self-esteem issues that affect how you speak.

Healing Practices:

Assertiveness Exercises: Practice asserting your needs and desires with confidence. Start with small situations where you can express yourself clearly and stand your ground.

Affirmations: "I express my truth with confidence."

Solar Plexus Stones: Use Citrine, Tiger's Eye, or Yellow Jasper to strengthen personal power and clarity in your communication.

4. Heart Chakra and Communication

Focus: Compassion, Empathy, and Loving Expression

The Heart Chakra (Anahata) governs love, compassion, and emotional connection, which are key components of meaningful communication.

Impact on Communication: A balanced Heart Chakra enhances your ability to communicate with empathy, compassion, and openness. It allows you to listen actively and speak from a place of love, which deepens connections with others.

Imbalance Symptoms: If the Heart Chakra is blocked, you may find it difficult to express love or care through words. You might also struggle with forgiveness or feel emotionally distant, making communication less open and authentic.

Healing Practices:

Empathetic Listening: Practice listening to others with full attention, without judgment, and with compassion.

Loving Speech: Speak with kindness and patience, ensuring that your words reflect love, understanding, and compassion.

Heart Chakra Stones: Use Rose Quartz, Green Aventurine, or Malachite to foster compassionate communication and emotional healing.

5. Throat Chakra and Communication

Focus: Expression, Truth, and Verbal Communication

The Throat Chakra (Vishuddha) is directly associated with all forms of communication, including speaking your truth and listening to others.

Impact on Communication: A balanced Throat Chakra helps you express yourself clearly, authentically, and with ease. It allows you to speak your truth, communicate your ideas, and listen attentively to others.

Imbalance Symptoms: If the Throat Chakra is blocked, you may struggle with speaking up for yourself, expressing your needs, or communicating your thoughts clearly. You might also feel misunderstood or unable to listen actively to others.

Healing Practices:

Affirmative Speech: Practice speaking your truth by expressing your thoughts and feelings honestly. Engage in conversations where you can speak freely and listen without interrupting.

Breathwork: Incorporate deep breathing exercises to calm your mind and prepare your body for clear verbal expression.

Throat Chakra Stones: Use Aquamarine, Blue Lace Agate, or Sodalite to enhance clear and honest communication.

6. Third Eye Chakra and Communication

Focus: Intuition, Insight, and Understanding

The Third Eye Chakra (Ajna) governs intuition and the ability to see the deeper truths behind situations. It aids in both verbal and non-verbal communication.

Impact on Communication: When the Third Eye Chakra is balanced, you can communicate with insight, intuition, and clarity. You are able to read between the lines and understand not only the words but also the emotions and intentions behind them.

Imbalance Symptoms: If the Third Eye Chakra is blocked, you may struggle with understanding others' feelings or motivations. Your communication may become overly logical, missing the deeper emotional layers of a conversation.

Healing Practices:

Intuitive Listening: Practice listening beyond words. Pay attention to non-verbal cues such as body language, tone, and energy.

Mindful Communication: Take a moment to reflect before speaking, allowing yourself to tune into your intuition to ensure that your words are aligned with your deeper understanding.

Third Eye Stones: Use Amethyst, Lapis Lazuli, or Fluorite to enhance intuitive communication and clarity in your interactions.

7. Crown Chakra and Communication

Focus: Spiritual Connection, Higher Truth, and Universal Love

The Crown Chakra (Sahasrara) governs our connection to divine wisdom and the universal truths that transcend individual perspectives.

Impact on Communication: A balanced Crown Chakra allows you to communicate from a place of spiritual understanding and universal love. You may find yourself speaking with wisdom, compassion, and a sense of unity with others.

Imbalance Symptoms: If the Crown Chakra is blocked, you may experience disconnection from the broader truth or feel isolated in your communication. Your words may lack depth or alignment with your higher purpose.

Healing Practices:

Meditative Listening: Engage in deep listening that connects you to the greater spiritual truth behind words. Meditate on the interconnectedness of all beings.

Divine Expression: Allow your communication to reflect your higher self and spiritual understanding, speaking with humility and grace.

Crown Chakra Stones: Use Clear Quartz, Selenite, or Amethyst to promote spiritual connection and higher wisdom in communication.

General Tips for Enhancing Communication Through the Chakras:

1. Mindfulness: Practice mindfulness in your communication by being fully present and engaged, both in speaking and listening.

2. Non-Verbal Cues: Pay attention to body language, tone of voice, and other non-verbal signals that influence the effectiveness of communication.

3. Energy Work: Regularly practice energy healing techniques, such as meditation, breathwork, and chakra balancing, to improve your overall communication abilities.

4. Clear Intentions: Before engaging in a conversation, set an intention to communicate clearly, respectfully, and truthfully.

CHAPTER XXXI

PRACTICES OF ASANA, PRANAYAMA

Chakras, yogasanas (yoga poses), and pranayama (breathing techniques) are powerful tools in the practice of energy healing and spiritual awakening. Each chakra governs specific aspects of our physical, mental, emotional, and spiritual health, and yogaasanas and pranayama can help activate, balance, and harmonize these energy centers.

1. Root Chakra (Muladhara)

Element: Earth

Color: Red

Location: Base of the spine, tailbone area

Associated Qualities: Safety, stability, grounding, physical health, survival instincts

Yogasanas for Root Chakra:

To activate and balance the root chakra, grounding poses that focus on stability, strength, and connection to the Earth are key. These poses help you feel more centered and connected to your body.

- **Tadasana (Mountain Pose):**
    - Stand tall with feet together, grounding through your feet.
    - Stretch your hands upwards, interlock fingers, and lengthen the spine.
    - Focus on the connection to the earth.
    - Feel your feet firmly grounded and visualize roots connecting you to the earth.
- **Vrikshasana (Tree Pose):**

- Stand on one leg and rest the sole of the other foot against your inner thigh.
- Join palms at the chest or overhead.
- Cultivate balance and stability.

Pranayama for Root Chakra:

The root chakra is deeply connected to the body and breath. Pranayama practices that focus on grounding, calming, and centering are ideal.

- **Deep Belly Breathing:**

  - Sit comfortably and breathe deeply into your abdomen.
  - Visualize a red glow at the base of your spine expanding with every breath.
  - Deep belly breathing, 10 breaths.

2. Sacral Chakra (Svadhisthana)

Element: Water

Color: Orange

Location: Lower abdomen, two inches below the navel closer to the reproductive organ.

Associated Qualities: Creativity, sensuality, pleasure, emotional expression, relationships

Yogasanas for Sacral Chakra:

To stimulate the sacral chakra, asanas that involve fluid movements and open the hips, pelvis, and lower abdomen can enhance creativity and emotional release.

- **Baddha Konasana (Bound Angle Pose):**

  - Sit on the floor, bring the soles of your feet together, and hold your feet with your hands.
  - Gently press your knees toward the ground, breathing into your hips.

- **Upavistha Konasana (Wide-Angle Seated Forward Bend):**
    - Sit with legs spread wide, hinge forward, and stretch your arms outward.
    - Lean forward and relax into the pose.

Pranayàma for Sacral Chakra:

Breathing techniques that involve deep, flowing breaths can help open the sacral chakra, encouraging emotional release and creative energy.

- **Nadi Shodhana (Alternate Nostril Breathing):**
    - Close the right nostril with your thumb, inhale through the left.
    - Close the left nostril with your ring finger, exhale through the right.
    - Imagine an orange light glowing in your lower abdomen.
    - Repeat for 5–10 minutes, balancing energy flow.

3. Solar Plexus Chakra (Manipura)

Element: Fire

Color: Yellow

Location: Upper abdomen, near the diaphragm

Associated Qualities: Personal power, confidence, willpower, self-esteem, transformation

Yogasanas for Solar Plexus Chakra:

The solar plexus chakra thrives with poses that strengthen the core, boost personal power, and enhance confidence.

- **Navasana (Boat Pose):**
    - Sit with knees bent and lift your legs, forming a V-shape with your body.
    - Extend your arms parallel to the floor and engage your core.

  - Engage your core and feel strength radiating.
  - Hold for 30 seconds, rest, and repeat 2–3 times.

- **Dhanurasana (Bow Pose):**

  - Lie on your stomach, bend your knees towards your buttocks and firmly hold your ankles.
  - Lift your chest and thighs, creating a bow shape.
  - Hold for 30 seconds, rest, and repeat 2–3 times.

Pranayama for Solar Plexus Chakra:

Breathing exercises that ignite the fire element, energize the core, and improve mental clarity are beneficial for the solar plexus.

- **Kapalabhati (Skull Shining Breath):**

  - Take a deep inhale, then exhale forcefully through the nose while contracting your abdomen.
  - Continue rhythmic exhales for 1–2 minutes.
  - Feel your belly energizing with each lift.
  - Hold for 20–30 seconds, repeat twice.

4. Heart Chakra (Anahata)

Element: Air

Color: Green or Pink

Location: Center of the chest, near the heart

Associated Qualities: Love, compassion, healing, forgiveness, empathy, connection

Yogasanas for Heart Chakra:

Heart-opening poses that stretch the chest and shoulders are essential to activate and heal the heart chakra.

Yogasanas:

- **Ustrasana (Camel Pose):**

- Kneel and arch your back, bringing your hands to your heels.
- Open your chest and lift your heart space.
- Open your chest and focus on love and compassion.
- Hold for 20–30 seconds, repeat twice.

- **Bhujangasana (Cobra Pose):**
    - Lie on your stomach and place hands beneath your shoulders.
    - Press up, lifting your chest and opening the heart.
    - Let your heart space lift and expand.
    - Hold for 30 seconds, repeat twice.

Pranayama for Heart Chakra:

Breathing techniques that calm the nervous system, promote openness, and cultivate compassion are ideal for the heart chakra.

- **Anulom Vilom (Alternate Nostril Breathing):**
    - Similar to Nadi Shodhana but focus on a green light emanating and expanding from your chest as you breathe.
    - Close the right nostril with your thumb, inhale through the left.
    - Close the left nostril with your ring finger, exhale through the right.
    - Alternate this practice for 5 minutes .

5. Throat Chakra (Vishuddha)

Element: Ether (Space)

Color: Blue

Location: Throat

Associated Qualities: Communication, self-expression, truth, creativity, listening

Yogasanas for Throat Chakra:

To open the throat chakra, poses that stretch the neck, shoulders, and throat, as well as those that encourage vocal expression, are beneficial.

- **Matsyasana (Fish Pose):**
    - Lie on your back and arch your upper spine, letting the crown of your head touch the ground.
    - Place hands under your hips for support.
    - Feel your throat open and relaxed.
    - Hold for 1 minute.
- **Simhasana (Lion's Pose):**
    - Sit on your knees, lean forward, and place your palms on the floor.
    - Inhale deeply, then exhale while roaring like a lion, sticking out your tongue.
    - Let go of any tension with the roaring exhale.
    - Repeat 3–5 times.

Pranayama for Throat Chakra:
Breathing exercises that promote vocal expression and clear communication are essential for this chakra.

- **Ujjayi (Ocean Breath):**
    - Constrict the back of your throat as you breathe, producing a soft, ocean-like sound.
    - Visualize blue light radiating from your throat.
    - Ujjayi (Ocean Breath) for 2–3 minutes.

6. Third Eye Chakra (Ajna)
Element: Light
Color: Indigo
Location: Between the eyebrows, center of the forehead

Associated Qualities: Intuition, wisdom, perception, inner vision, clarity

Yogasanas for Third Eye Chakra:

The third eye chakra benefits from practices that stimulate the mind, intuition, and inner sight.

- **Balasana (Child's Pose):**
    - Sit on your heels and fold forward, resting your forehead on the floor.
    - Feel the pressure at your third eye.
    - Rest for 2 minutes, forehead touching the ground.
- **Ardha Pincha Mayurasana (Dolphin Pose):**
    - From a plank, lift your hips and rest on your forearms, pressing your forehead gently down.
    - Direct your gaze inward.
    - Hold for 30 seconds, repeat twice.

Pranayama for Third Eye Chakra:

Breathing techniques that clear the mind, enhance focus, and improve intuition are ideal for stimulating the third eye.

- **Bhramari (Bee Breath):**
    - Inhale deeply, then exhale while humming like a bee.
    - Focus on vibrations and visualize an indigo light at your forehead.

7. Crown Chakra (Sahasrara)
Element: Thought
Color: Violet or White
Location: Top of the head

Associated Qualities: Spirituality, enlightenment, connection to higher consciousness

Yogasanas for Crown Chakra:

To activate the crown chakra, poses that encourage connection to the divine and higher consciousness are helpful.

- **Savasana (Corpse Pose):**
  - Lie flat on your back, letting your body relax completely.
  - Imagine white or violet light connecting you to the universe.
  - Rest for 5–10 minutes.
- **Padmasana (Lotus Pose):**
  - Sit cross-legged, placing each foot on the opposite thigh.
  - Keep your spine erect and focus on your crown.
  - Visualize energy flowing upward to your crown.
  - Sit for 2–3 minutes.

Pranayama for Crown Chakra:

Breathing techniques that focus on stillness, surrender, and connection to the divine help balance the crown chakra.

- **Silent Meditation:**
  - Silent meditation on breath or mantra ("Om") for 5 minutes.
  - Focus on your breath, imagining a violet or white light above your head connecting you to higher consciousness.

Notes for Practice:

1. **The duration of practice mentioned, do consider it has suggestion only.**
2. **Dont hurt yourself, take it easy.**

3. Hold poses for a duration that feels comfortable, increasing as you gain strength and flexibility.
4. Always move mindfully and focus on your breath.
5. Start and End with gratitude for the practice.

CHAPTER XXXII

CHAKRAS - SYSTEMS OF THE BODY

Asana (physical postures) and pranayama (breath control) are integral parts of yoga that not only benefit the musculoskeletal system but also have profound effects on all the major systems of the body. Both asanas and pranayama are designed to optimize the flow of energy (prana) and balance the body and mind, creating harmony across the physical, mental, and energetic planes. Below is an exploration of how specific asanas and pranayama can influence various systems of the body.

1. Musculoskeletal System

Asanas: Regular practice of asanas strengthens, stretches, and aligns the bones, joints, and muscles. For example:

Downward Dog (Adho Mukha Svanasana): Strengthens the arms, legs, and back.

Tree Pose (Vrikshasana): Improves balance, strengthens the legs and core.

Cobra Pose (Bhujangasana): Strengthens the spine and relieves back pain.

Pranayama: Kapalabhati (skull shining breath) and Bhastrika (bellows breath) can activate energy and oxygenate tissues, supporting muscle recovery and joint flexibility.

2. Cardiovascular System

Asanas: Certain asanas stimulate blood flow and improve heart function. For example:

Warrior Poses (Virabhadrasana I, II, III): Increase cardiovascular endurance and improve heart function.

Camel Pose (Ustrasana): Opens the chest and expands the lungs, improving circulation and oxygenation.

Bridge Pose (Setu Bandhasana): Stimulates the heart, improves circulation, and strengthens the lower body.

Pranayama:

Anulom Vilom (Nadi Shodhana, alternate nostril breathing) helps calm the nervous system, regulate blood pressure, and improve circulation.

Ujjayi Breath (victorious breath) enhances circulation, reduces heart rate, and helps with focus and endurance during physical activities.

3. Respiratory System

Asanas: Certain asanas expand the lungs and increase lung capacity:

Fish Pose (Matsyasana): Opens up the chest, improving lung function and capacity.

Cat-Cow Pose (Marjaryasana-Bitilasana): Encourages deep breathing and expansion of the diaphragm.

Seated Forward Fold (Paschimottanasana): Stretches the back and opens the lungs, helping improve breath control.

Pranayama:

Bhastrika (bellows breath) increases lung capacity and clears the respiratory passages, improving oxygen intake.

Kapalabhati (skull shining breath) and Anulom Vilom promote deep, rhythmic breathing and help detoxify the lungs.

Bhramari (bee breath) helps release stress and clears the airways, supporting the respiratory system.

4. Digestive System

Asanas: Specific asanas stimulate the digestive organs, improve metabolism, and promote the elimination of toxins:

Twist Poses (Ardha Matsyendrasana, Bharadvajasana): Help massage the internal organs, aiding digestion and detoxification.

Seated Forward Fold (Paschimottanasana): Stimulates the digestive organs and helps relieve constipation.

Bow Pose (Dhanurasana): Massages the abdominal organs, stimulating digestion and metabolism.

Pranayama:

Kapalabhati helps to detoxify and energize the digestive organs by increasing blood flow to the digestive system.

Ujjayi Breath can help calm the digestive tract and reduce symptoms of indigestion and bloating.

Anulom Vilom (alternate nostril breathing) enhances oxygen flow to the body, improving digestion by supporting parasympathetic nervous function.

5. Endocrine System

Asanas: Asanas help regulate the endocrine system by stimulating and balancing various glandular functions:

Shoulder Stand (Sarvangasana): Stimulates the thyroid and parathyroid glands, balancing metabolism.

Plow Pose (Halasana): Stimulates the pituitary and thyroid glands, helping regulate hormonal activity.

Cobra Pose (Bhujangasana): Stimulates the adrenal glands, balancing stress hormones like cortisol.

Pranayama:

Kundalini Pranayama and Bhastrika help activate energy centers, promoting the flow of energy through the endocrine glands.

Anulom Vilom helps calm the nervous system, balancing hormonal secretion, and promoting relaxation and energy equilibrium.

6. Nervous System

Asanas: Many asanas calm the nervous system by promoting relaxation and mental clarity:

Child's Pose (Balasana): Relaxes the nervous system and calms the mind, relieving stress.

Legs Up the Wall (Viparita Karani): A restorative pose that reduces tension and promotes relaxation.

Corpse Pose (Savasana): Helps integrate the effects of practice and induces deep relaxation for the nervous system.

Pranayama:

Ujjayi Breath has a calming effect on the nervous system and helps reduce stress and anxiety.

Bhramari (bee breath) helps reduce stress and calm the mind, benefiting the sympathetic nervous system.

Nadi Shodhana (alternate nostril breathing) balances the left and right hemispheres of the brain and calms the nervous system.

7. Lymphatic System

Asanas: Yoga helps stimulate lymphatic circulation and supports detoxification:

Inversions (e.g., Headstand, Shoulder Stand): Aid in lymphatic drainage and stimulate the immune system.

Twisting poses (e.g., Half Lord of the Fishes Pose - Ardha Matsyendrasana) help flush toxins and activate lymph nodes.

Forward bends and standing poses stimulate lymphatic flow and improve circulation.

Pranayama:

Kapalabhati (skull shining breath) helps cleanse the lymphatic system by stimulating internal detoxification.

Anulom Vilom and Ujjayi breath help oxygenate tissues and promote the flow of lymph through the body.

8. Immune System

Asanas: Certain yoga poses help stimulate the immune system, enhance circulation, and reduce inflammation:

Downward Dog (Adho Mukha Svanasana): Improves circulation and immune function by stimulating the lymphatic system.

Warrior Poses (Virabhadrasana): Increase stamina, promote strength, and boost immune system function.

Pranayama:

Kapalabhati (skull shining breath) and Bhastrika (bellows breath) invigorate the body and increase energy, boosting immune function.

Anulom Vilom promotes relaxation and helps regulate sympathetic nervous activity, supporting immune responses and stress management.

9. Urinary System

Asanas: Certain asanas stimulate the kidneys and bladder, improving their function:

Child's Pose (Balasana): Helps release tension in the lower back, aiding kidney function.

Bow Pose (Dhanurasana): Massages the abdominal organs, stimulating the kidneys.

Twists (e.g., Seated Twist) stimulate the bladder and kidneys, aiding detoxification.

Pranayama:

Bhastrika breath invigorates the kidneys and promotes fluid balance.

Anulom Vilom helps balance the nervous system and relieve urinary retention or incontinence issues.

10. Reproductive System

Asanas: Yoga poses stimulate the pelvic area and promote the health of the reproductive organs:

Bound Angle Pose (Baddha Konasana): Improves circulation to the pelvic area and supports reproductive health.

Cat-Cow Pose (Marjaryasana-Bitilasana): Stimulates the reproductive organs and improves the flexibility of the spine and hips.

Child's Pose (Balasana): A calming pose that relieves stress, benefiting the reproductive organs.

Pranayama:

Kundalini Pranayama activates the pelvic region, enhancing sexual energy and promoting the health of the reproductive system.

Ujjayi Breath helps to reduce stress, balancing the hormones that regulate reproductive health.

11. Skeletal System

Asanas: Asanas strengthen the bones, improve posture, and increase bone density:

Mountain Pose (Tadasana): Strengthens the bones and improves posture, promoting skeletal alignment.

Warrior I (Virabhadrasana I): Strengthens bones, particularly in the legs and spine.

Triangle Pose (Trikonasana): Increases flexibility and strengthens the bones, especially in the spine and hips.

Pranayama:

Ujjayi Breath can help strengthen bones and balance the energy flow that affects the skeletal system.

12. Exocrine System and Yoga

The exocrine system includes glands that secrete substances like sweat, saliva, digestive enzymes, and breast milk into ducts that lead to external or internal body surfaces. Major exocrine glands include:

Salivary glands

Sweat glands

Mammary glands

Pancreas (secretes digestive enzymes into the intestines)

Liver (secretes bile into the digestive tract)

Both asana and pranayama can play a significant role in stimulating and supporting the function of these glands, promoting secretion and balance.

Asanas for the Exocrine System

Salivary Glands:

Simhasana (Lion's Pose): This pose stimulates the throat and encourages deep breathing, promoting the flow of saliva and improving throat health.

Cobra Pose (Bhujangasana): Helps open the throat, promoting circulation and stimulating the salivary glands.

Sweat Glands:

Downward Dog (Adho Mukha Svanasana): Encourages circulation and can promote sweating due to the inversion, which helps detoxify the body.

Twisting Poses: Twists like Ardha Matsyendrasana stimulate the body's detoxification process, encouraging the excretion of sweat and toxins.

Mammary Glands:

Camel Pose (Ustrasana): Opens the chest and stimulates the mammary glands by expanding the ribcage.

Bridge Pose (Setu Bandhasana): This backbend also stimulates the chest area, enhancing circulation to the mammary glands.

Fish Pose (Matsyasana): Also a chest opener, supporting the hormonal balance related to lactation and mammary gland function.

Pancreas:

Seated Forward Fold (Paschimottanasana): This deep forward bend massages the abdomen, stimulating the pancreas and promoting healthy digestive enzyme production.

Bow Pose (Dhanurasana): Stretches and stimulates the abdominal area, supporting pancreas function and digestive enzyme secretion.

Liver and Gallbladder (Bile Secretion):

Revolved Triangle Pose (Parivrtta Trikonasana): Helps stimulate the abdominal organs, supporting bile secretion and liver health.

Twists: Poses like Marichyasana and Ardha Matsyendrasana can help detoxify the body and encourage proper secretion from the liver.

Pranayama for the Exocrine System

Salivary Glands:

Kapalabhati (Skull Shining Breath): This pranayama technique increases circulation to the face and head, promoting the secretion of saliva and stimulating digestion.

Bhramari (Bee Breath): This calming breath can help activate the throat and stimulate salivary production by relaxing the facial muscles and promoting deeper respiration.

Sweat Glands:

Sitali Pranayama (Cooling Breath): This pranayama cools the body, activating sweat glands in the process and promoting a sense of relaxation while helping in body temperature regulation.

Ujjayi Pranayama (Victorious Breath): While primarily calming, it also can support detoxification, leading to improved sweat flow when combined with asana practices.

Pancreas and Digestion:

Bhastrika Pranayama (Bellows Breath): Increases oxygen flow to the abdominal area, improving the secretion of digestive enzymes from the pancreas and enhancing digestion.

Anulom Vilom (Alternate Nostril Breathing): Helps balance the nervous system, indirectly supporting the digestive process by calming stress, which can affect pancreatic function.

Liver and Gallbladder:

Kapalabhati and Bhastrika can stimulate the liver and help the secretion of bile by increasing circulation to the abdominal area.

Anulom Vilom helps with stress management, supporting the liver in detoxifying the body.

Summary of Asana and Pranayama Effects on the Exocrine System:

Salivary Glands: Asanas like Simhasana and Cobra Pose, along with pranayama techniques like Kapalabhati and Bhramari, help stimulate the production of saliva and improve throat health.

Sweat Glands: Asanas such as Downward Dog and twisting poses, along with Sitali Pranayama, promote sweating and help detoxify the body.

Mammary Glands: Poses like Camel Pose and Fish Pose, combined with pranayama like Bhramari, support lactation and hormonal balance in the mammary glands.

Pancreas: Asanas like Paschimottanasana and Bow Pose, along with Bhastrika pranayama, stimulate pancreatic function and improve digestion.

Liver and Gallbladder: Twisting poses like Revolved Triangle Pose and pranayama techniques like Kapalabhati help stimulate bile production and liver detoxification.

13.Integumentary System and Yoga

The integumentary system serves as a protective barrier for the body, regulating temperature, and preventing infections. It consists primarily of the skin, hair, nails, sweat glands, and sebaceous glands. Regular yoga practice, through both asana and pranayama, can significantly improve circulation, promote detoxification, enhance skin health, and stimulate hair and nail growth.

Asanas for the Integumentary System

Skin Health:

Downward Dog (Adho Mukha Svanasana): This inversion enhances blood circulation to the face and head, promoting a healthy complexion and glowing skin by encouraging the detoxification process.

Cobra Pose (Bhujangasana): Improves circulation to the skin, especially around the chest and face, and helps open the chest, which can reduce skin congestion and acne.

Plow Pose (Halasana): An inversion that stimulates the entire body, improving blood flow to the skin and aiding in detoxification.

Bridge Pose (Setu Bandhasana): Promotes circulation to the upper body and face, nourishing the skin and improving its appearance by promoting detoxification and oxygenation.

Hair Health:

Forward Folds (e.g., Paschimottanasana): Increases circulation to the scalp, supporting hair growth by encouraging the flow of oxygen and nutrients to hair follicles.

Child's Pose (Balasana): A restorative pose that relaxes the body and reduces stress, which can help prevent hair loss related to tension or anxiety.

Nail Health:

Mountain Pose (Tadasana): Helps improve posture and circulation to the extremities, supporting healthy nails.

Warrior I (Virabhadrasana I): Strengthens the arms and hands, encouraging better circulation to the nails and improving overall hand health.

Tree Pose (Vrikshasana): Balances energy and promotes grounding, supporting overall vitality, including nail growth and health.

Detoxification (Sweat Glands):

Twist Poses (e.g., Ardha Matsyendrasana): Help stimulate the digestive system and encourage the flow of sweat, promoting detoxification through the skin.

Puppy Pose (Uttana Shishosana): This pose opens up the chest and abdomen, aiding the sweat glands in the detoxification process by increasing circulation and promoting healthy sweat production.

Pranayama for the Integumentary System

Improving Circulation to the Skin:

Ujjayi Pranayama (Victorious Breath): This technique helps calm the nervous system, which can reduce stress-related skin issues like acne or eczema. It also increases blood flow, nourishing the skin.

Kapalabhati (Skull Shining Breath): By increasing oxygen flow to the head and face, Kapalabhati can rejuvenate the skin and give it a radiant glow. It also stimulates the removal of toxins from the body, benefiting skin health.

Anulom Vilom (Alternate Nostril Breathing): This balancing pranayama can help reduce stress, which can otherwise negatively impact the skin. It also encourages detoxification through deep, even breathing, improving skin clarity and vibrancy.

Detoxification:

Bhastrika (Bellows Breath): Increases circulation and oxygen levels in the body, promoting detoxification through the skin and improving the quality of skin by enhancing lymphatic drainage and removing toxins.

Shitali Pranayama (Cooling Breath): This pranayama cools the body, which can help calm irritated skin or conditions like acne or rosacea. It also stimulates the sweat glands and aids in the detoxification process.

Hair and Scalp Health:

Kapalabhati can stimulate the scalp, increasing blood flow and promoting the release of impurities, which is beneficial for hair health.

Bhramari (Bee Breath): The vibrations created by this pranayama can relax the mind and reduce stress, which is often a factor in hair loss. It also calms thc body and helps release tension in the scalp, improving circulation to the hair follicles.

Key Benefits of Asanas and Pranayama for the Integumentary System:

Skin:

Regular asana practice increases blood circulation, delivering essential nutrients and oxygen to the skin, promoting a healthy and youthful appearance.

Pranayama like Kapalabhati and Ujjayi Breath help detoxify the body, clearing the skin from within by expelling toxins through sweat and breath.

Hair:

Forward Fold, increase blood flow to the scalp, which nourishes hair follicles and promotes growth.

Breathwork, such as Kapalabhati, encourages the flow of oxygen and energy to the scalp, supporting strong, healthy hair.

Nails:

Asanas that strengthen the arms and promote circulation, like Tadasana and Virabhadrasana I, ensure nutrients reach the nails, contributing to their health and growth.

Sweat Glands:

Poses like Downward Dog and Twists stimulate sweat production, helping detoxify the body and clear the pores, which is essential for maintaining healthy skin.

Pranayama techniques like Bhastrika promote sweat flow and encourage the release of toxins from the body, supporting skin clarity and overall detoxification.

In conclusion, asana and pranayama work synergistically to benefit and balance all systems of the body. Through conscious movement and breathing techniques, yoga offers a comprehensive approach to physical health and emotional well-being, promoting vitality, flexibility, and stress reduction across every body system.

CHAPTER XXXIII

CHAKRAS AND AROMATHERAPY

Aromatherapy is the practice of using essential oils extracted from plants to enhance physical, emotional, and spiritual well-being. These oils are typically inhaled, applied topically (often diluted with a carrier oil), or used in diffusers. Each essential oil has a specific energetic vibration that can support the balancing and healing of the chakra system.

Aromatherapy can help balance and align the chakras by addressing the emotional, mental, and physical imbalances that can arise when the energy in a particular chakra becomes blocked or out of alignment. Certain essential oils resonate with the frequencies of the different chakras, promoting healing and restoring balance.

Aromatherapy offers a powerful tool for supporting chakra healing by using the therapeutic properties of essential oils to restore balance to the body's energy centers. By understanding the qualities of different essential oils and their relationship to each chakra, you can customize your aromatherapy practice to enhance emotional healing, self-awareness, and spiritual connection. Whether through diffusion, topical application, or inhalation, essential oils can help align, open, and balance the chakras, contributing to overall well-being.

1. Root Chakra (Muladhara) – Stability and Grounding

Location: Base of the spine, near the tailbone.

Function: The Root Chakra governs survival, stability, grounding, and security. When balanced, it provides a sense of safety, stability, and connection to the Earth.

Emotional Imbalances: Fear, anxiety, insecurity, financial or survival worries.

Essential Oils:

Vetiver: Deeply grounding, it supports feelings of stability and security.

Patchouli: Known for its earthy scent, patchouli helps reconnect with the body and brings grounding energy.

Sandalwood: Promotes calm, grounding, and inner strength.

Cedarwood: Encourages emotional stability and a sense of rootedness.

Frankincense: Encourages grounding, helping you stay centered in challenging times.

How to Use: Diffuse in the home or apply diluted to the lower back or soles of the feet.

2. Sacral Chakra (Svadhisthana) – Creativity and Emotions

Location: Lower abdomen, about two inches below the navel.

Function: This chakra is related to creativity, emotions, relationships, and pleasure. A balanced Sacral Chakra promotes emotional flow, healthy relationships, and a vibrant creative life.

Emotional Imbalances: Guilt, shame, emotional instability, creative blocks, sexual issues.

Essential Oils:

Ylang Ylang: Promotes emotional balance, passion, and openness in relationships.

Jasmine: Enhances creativity, self-expression, and sexual energy.

Sweet Orange: Uplifts the mood and encourages emotional openness.

Clary Sage: Supports emotional healing and balances hormones.

Rose: Helps foster love, emotional balance, and connection.

How to Use: Diffuse in a creative space, or apply diluted to the lower abdomen to support emotional release and creativity.

3. Solar Plexus Chakra (Manipura) – Personal Power and Confidence

Location: Upper abdomen, above the navel.

Function: The Solar Plexus Chakra is the center of personal power, confidence, self-esteem, and willpower. When balanced, it helps you feel empowered, confident, and capable of taking action.

Emotional Imbalances: Low self-esteem, lack of confidence, indecisiveness, anger issues.

Essential Oils:

Lemon: Refreshes and boosts clarity, mental focus, and self-confidence.

Ginger: Stimulates vitality, confidence, and strength.

Coriander: Promotes clarity, personal power, and mental sharpness.

Peppermint: Energizes and enhances focus, helping overcome mental fatigue.

Bergamot: Uplifts mood, reduces anxiety, and helps boost self-confidence.

How to Use: Diffuse in your workspace to promote confidence, or massage diluted oil on the abdomen to support personal empowerment.

4. Heart Chakra (Anahata) – Love and Compassion

Location: Center of the chest, near the heart.

Function: The Heart Chakra governs love, compassion, empathy, and forgiveness. When balanced, it opens you to giving and receiving love, fostering healthy relationships.

Emotional Imbalances: Grief, jealousy, emotional pain, difficulty giving or receiving love.

Essential Oils:

Rose: The quintessential oil for love, emotional healing, and compassion.

Geranium: Encourages emotional balance and openness in relationships.

Lavender: Calms and soothes the heart, promoting inner peace and emotional healing.

Rosemary: Supports healing from emotional wounds and grief.

Basil: Clears emotional congestion, supporting forgiveness and compassion.

How to Use: Use in a diffuser to promote love and calm, or apply diluted oil over the chest area to open the heart.

5. Throat Chakra (Vishuddha) – Communication and Expression

Location: Throat area.

Function: The Throat Chakra is associated with communication, self-expression, and speaking your truth. When balanced, it enables clear and honest expression.

Emotional Imbalances: Difficulty expressing yourself, fear of speaking, feeling misunderstood.

Essential Oils:

Eucalyptus: Clears the throat and opens channels for clear communication.

Peppermint: Helps clear the mind and facilitates the expression of ideas.

Chamomile: Calms the throat and enhances the ability to speak with compassion and clarity.

Tea Tree: Promotes clarity of communication and protects from negative energy.

Lavender: Promotes calmness and ease, reducing anxiety around self-expression.

How to Use: Apply diluted oil to the throat area or diffuse during conversations or public speaking to support clear communication.

6. Third Eye Chakra (Ajna) – Intuition and Clarity

Location: Between the eyebrows, and on the forehead.

Function: The Third Eye Chakra is associated with intuition, insight, and spiritual awareness. A balanced Third Eye Chakra enables clear vision, intuition, and access to higher wisdom.

Emotional Imbalances: Confusion, lack of clarity, feeling disconnected from intuition.

Essential Oils:

Frankincense: Elevates spiritual awareness, enhancing insight and clarity.

Sandalwood: Grounding and calming, it supports intuitive awareness and mental clarity.

Clary Sage: Helps open the mind to intuition and higher consciousness.

Lavender: Calms the mind, promoting mental clarity and insight.

Patchouli: Grounds the energy while enhancing intuitive awareness.

How to Use: Apply diluted oil between the eyebrows or diffuse during meditation to enhance intuition and clarity.

7. Crown Chakra (Sahasrara) – Spiritual Connection and Enlightenment

Location: Top of the head.

Function: The Crown Chakra is the center of spiritual connection, enlightenment, and higher consciousness. When balanced, it promotes a sense of divine connection, peace, and wisdom.

Emotional Imbalances: Feeling disconnected from spirituality, lack of purpose, confusion.

Essential Oils:

Lavender: Promotes spiritual awakening and inner peace.

Rosemary: Stimulates the mind and enhances spiritual clarity.

Frankincense: Elevates the spirit, encourages meditation, and enhances higher consciousness.

Jasmine: Enhances spiritual awareness and supports emotional balance.

Sandalwood: Helps connect to higher consciousness and encourages divine insight.

How to Use: Use in a diffuser during meditation to enhance spiritual connection, or apply diluted oil to the top of the head for grounding and spiritual clarity.

METHODS OF USING NATURAL ESSENTIAL OILS

Aromatic Baths: sprinkle 4-8 drops of essential oil onto the water's surface after the bath has been drawn. Agitate the water to disperse the oil. Neat essences never leave a greasy tide mark due to their tiny molecular structure. The effect of such baths is to reduce tension in the body and mind.

Aromatic Toweling: after washing as usual, put 2-3 drops of your favorite essential oil on a wet face cloth or sponge; run it briskly all over your body.

Atomisers: use a small garden pump or a spray bottle to disperse the molecules (dilute in rose water for best results) into the air in a fine mist.

Cotton Ball: Add a few drops of essential oil to a cotton ball in a small bowl and let it slowly disperse the oil into the air; this is suitable for wardrobes, traveling, office desks, and automobiles.

Cream and Shampoo: to enhance the therapeutic effect of your favorite cream or shampoo add a drop of suitable essential oil and feel the difference.

Diffuser: To get the most from your Essential Oils a Diffuser is used to help disperse the molecules into the air. This enables the body to use them as you breathe in the wonderful aromas. Some use electricity and others use a heating element or a small lit candle under a bowl of water. In the bowl add water and a few drops of your favorite essential oil, the heat generated from the electricity or a lit candle will warm the water and help disperse the oil molecules into the air.

Foot and Hand Baths: sprinkle 5-6 drops of the appropriate essential oil in a bowl of lukewarm water. Soak your feet or hands for about 10 minutes. At the end of a tiring day, this can be relaxing and can even alleviate tension headaches.

Gargles and Mouthwashes: for sore throats and laryngitis add one drop of sandalwood or lemon or peppermint oil to a glass containing 2 teaspoonfuls of cider vinegar. Stir well to disperse the oil, and then fill the glass with warm water. Natural essential oil dissolves better in cedar vinegar than in water and also vinegar helps reduce the build-up of tartar on the backs of the teeth.

Inhalations: to help clear nasal passages when you have a cold or flu, put 5-10 drops of essential oil on your handkerchief and inhale as required. Essential oil can also be sprinkled on your pillow to ease nasal congestion and to aid restful sleep.

Neat Application: provided the skin is cooled first under cold running water for at least 5 minutes, lavender, eucalyptus, tea tree, or geranium can be applied neat to minor burns and scalds.

Steam Inhalations: pour 500 ml of near-boiling water into a bowl and then add 2-4 drops of essential oil. Inhale the vapors for 5-10 minutes. In order to trap the aromatic steam more effectively, drape a towel over your head and the bowl to form a tent. Steam inhalations help relieve respiratory problems or as deep–cleansing facials.

Compress: add about 6 drops of essential oil to a bowl containing about 500 ml of water, as hot as you can comfortably bear. Place a small towel on top of the water. Wring out the excess and place the towel over the area to be treated or run the town all over your body. A compress is a valuable way of treating muscular pain, sprains and bruises as well as reducing pain and congestion in internal organs.

CHAPTER XXXIV

CHAKRAS AND CBT

Cognitive Behavioral Therapy (CBT) is a popular therapeutic approach designed to help individuals identify and change negative thought patterns and behaviors that contribute to emotional and psychological distress. It focuses on the connection between thoughts, feelings, and behaviors and uses practical strategies to shift unhealthy patterns. Although CBT is primarily a psychological approach, it can complement chakra work by addressing the mental and emotional blockages that affect the flow of energy in the chakra system.

Cognitive Behavioral Therapy (CBT) can be a valuable tool for supporting chakra healing by addressing the negative thought patterns, beliefs, and behaviors that create blockages in the chakra system. By combining CBT with chakra work, individuals can achieve greater emotional, mental, and physical balance. This integrated approach helps release past emotional wounds, shift limiting beliefs, and enhance the flow of energy throughout the body, leading to lasting healing and personal growth.

Integrating CBT with chakra healing can be a powerful way to bring about lasting change by addressing both the psychological and energetic aspects of well-being.

How Cognitive Behavioral Therapy (CBT) Relates to Chakras:

CBT can be helpful in addressing the negative thought patterns, beliefs, and behaviors that create blockages in the chakras. By working with both the mental and emotional aspects of healing, CBT can enhance chakra healing in the following ways:

Identifying Negative Thought Patterns and Beliefs: Each chakra is associated with specific themes related to energy, such as survival, self-expression, personal power, and emotional balance. Negative thought patterns or limiting beliefs related to these themes can block the flow of energy in corresponding chakras. CBT helps identify these thought patterns, such as fears of abandonment (Root Chakra), self-doubt (Solar Plexus Chakra), or difficulty expressing one's truth (Throat Chakra), and provides tools to challenge and reframe them.

Transforming Negative Emotions: Negative emotions like fear, anger, guilt, or shame can accumulate in the body and become stored in the chakras. For instance, unresolved grief or resentment may block the Heart Chakra, while stress and anxiety may constrict the Root Chakra. CBT works by identifying the cognitive distortions that fuel these emotions and replacing them with healthier, more balanced perspectives. This process helps release emotional blockages, allowing energy to flow freely through the chakras.

Breaking Negative Behavioral Cycles: Negative behaviors and coping mechanisms (such as avoidance, self-sabotage, or overreaction) can manifest as blockages in the chakra system. For example, people with blocked Solar Plexus Chakras may struggle with setting boundaries or asserting themselves, while individuals with imbalances in the Sacral Chakra may have issues with healthy relationships or creativity. CBT helps individuals recognize and address these behaviors, which in turn supports the healing and balancing of the corresponding chakras.

Promoting Self-Awareness: One of the primary goals of CBT is increasing self-awareness and developing the ability to observe thoughts, feelings, and behaviors without judgment. This self-awareness is essential for chakra healing because it allows individuals to recognize when they are experiencing energetic imbalances, emotional triggers, or negative thought patterns. This awareness creates the space for healing and transformation, enabling individuals to align their thoughts and actions with the flow of energy in their chakras.

1. Root Chakra (Muladhara) – Grounding and Safety:
The Root Chakra is linked to survival instincts, safety, and security. When this chakra is blocked, individuals may experience anxiety, fear, or insecurity. CBT helps challenge irrational fears related to

survival and self-worth (e.g., fears of poverty, abandonment, or not being good enough). By identifying and reframing these thoughts, individuals can feel more grounded, stable, and secure, helping to balance the Root Chakra.

CBT Techniques: Thought records, reality testing, and reframing beliefs around security and survival.

2. Sacral Chakra (Svadhisthana) – Emotions and Creativity:
The Sacral Chakra governs emotions, relationships, and creativity. Blockages in this chakra may manifest as emotional instability, difficulty in relationships, or creative blocks. CBT can help individuals identify and challenge patterns of emotional reactivity or unhealthy relational patterns, such as codependency or avoidance. It also promotes healthier emotional regulation and creative expression by addressing underlying beliefs and behaviors.

CBT Techniques: Cognitive restructuring to address emotional triggers, mindfulness practices for emotional regulation, and exposure techniques for overcoming emotional avoidance.

3. Solar Plexus Chakra (Manipura) – Personal Power and Self-Esteem:
The Solar Plexus Chakra is associated with self-esteem, confidence, and personal power. When blocked, individuals may experience feelings of low self-worth, lack of motivation, or difficulty asserting themselves. CBT can help challenge negative beliefs about oneself and replace them with empowering thoughts. Techniques such as positive affirmations, self-compassion exercises, and setting achievable goals can help restore a sense of control and self-empowerment.

CBT Techniques: Self-affirmations, goal-setting, and addressing cognitive distortions such as all-or-nothing thinking or catastrophizing.

4. Heart Chakra (Anahata) – Love, Compassion, and Emotional Healing:
The Heart Chakra is central to love, compassion, and emotional healing. Blockages in this chakra often result from unresolved grief, heartbreak, or fear of intimacy. CBT can help individuals confront

and process past emotional wounds by addressing negative beliefs about love and relationships. By reframing thoughts of unworthiness, fear of rejection, or mistrust, individuals can open their hearts to healthier connections.

CBT Techniques: Grief processing, self-compassion, and challenging beliefs about love and trust.

5. Throat Chakra (Vishuddha) – Communication and Expression:

The Throat Chakra governs communication, self-expression, and speaking one's truth. When blocked, individuals may have difficulty speaking up, expressing their needs, or articulating their feelings. CBT helps individuals challenge fears of judgment or rejection that prevent them from expressing themselves authentically. It also helps confront any cognitive distortions around self-expression, such as the belief that one's voice is not important or valid.

CBT Techniques: Assertiveness training, exposure to situations that require communication, and challenging beliefs around self-expression.

6. Third Eye Chakra (Ajna) – Intuition and Clarity:

The Third Eye Chakra is responsible for intuition, insight, and clarity of thought. Blockages in this chakra may manifest as confusion, indecision, or difficulty trusting one's inner guidance. CBT can help individuals recognize and challenge the mental habits that lead to self-doubt and overthinking. Through mindfulness and cognitive reframing, individuals can develop greater clarity and trust in their intuition.

CBT Techniques: Mindfulness practices, cognitive reframing of self-doubt, and decision-making exercises.

7. Crown Chakra (Sahasrara) – Spiritual Connection and Purpose:

The Crown Chakra represents spiritual connection, higher consciousness, and a sense of purpose. Blockages in this chakra may result in feelings of spiritual emptiness, disconnection, or lack of purpose. CBT helps individuals confront limiting beliefs about spirituality, worthiness, or existential fears. By reframing these thoughts, individuals can experience a greater sense of connection to themselves, others, and the universe.

CBT Techniques: Cognitive reframing of existential beliefs, mindfulness, and exploring personal values and purpose.

Integrating CBT with Chakra Healing:

To maximize the benefits of both CBT and chakra healing, individuals can integrate the following practices:

1. Mindfulness Meditation: Cultivating mindfulness can help individuals observe their thoughts and feelings without judgment, which is a core component of CBT. Combining mindfulness with chakra meditation can help release emotional blockages stored in the body.

2. Visualization: During CBT sessions, individuals can visualize energy moving freely through each chakra as they work through negative thought patterns. This visualization can be a powerful tool to reinforce the healing process.

3. Breathwork: Using breathwork techniques alongside CBT can help release emotional tension, promote relaxation, and support chakra healing. Focused breathing can enhance self-awareness and allow individuals to connect with their energy system.

4. Affirmations and Reframing: Use positive affirmations that align with chakra healing to complement CBT techniques. For example, for the Root Chakra, affirmations like "I am safe and secure" can reinforce feelings of stability.

CHAPTER XXXV

CHAKRAS AND COLOURS

Chakras and color healing are deeply interconnected because each chakra is associated with a specific color that vibrates at a particular frequency. Color therapy, or chromotherapy, can be used to balance and energize the chakras by aligning their vibrational energy with the corresponding hues.

1. Root Chakra (Muladhara)

Color: Red

Meaning: Stability, security, grounding.

Healing with Color: Surround yourself with red hues through clothing, lighting, or visualization.

Suggestions: Use a red cloth during meditation, imagine red energy at the base of your spine, or spend time near red flowers or earthy tones.

Crystal: Red jasper, hematite.

2. Sacral Chakra (Svadhisthana)

Color: Orange

Meaning: Creativity, pleasure, emotional balance.

Healing with Color: Wear orange clothing or jewelry, light candles in warm orange shades, or visualize an orange glow in your lower abdomen.

Suggestions: Incorporate orange fruits like oranges or mangoes into your diet.

Crystal: Carnelian, moonstone.

3. Solar Plexus Chakra (Manipura)

Color: Yellow

Meaning: Confidence, willpower, personal power.

Healing with Color: Spend time in sunlight, wear yellow, or meditate with yellow crystals like citrine.

Suggestions: Visualize a radiant yellow sun at your solar plexus energizing and empowering you.

Crystal: Citrine, tiger's eye.

4. Heart Chakra (Anahata)

Color: Green (secondary: pink)

Meaning: Love, compassion, relationships.

Healing with Color: Decorate your space with green plants, wear green or pink clothing, and visualize a green light radiating from your heart.

Suggestions: Spend time in nature, focusing on greenery to connect with this chakra.

Crystal: Rose quartz, green aventurine.

5. Throat Chakra (Vishuddha)

Color: Blue (light blue)

Meaning: Communication, truth, self-expression.

Healing with Color: Meditate while wearing or holding blue gemstones (e.g., aquamarine), use blue lights, or drink water from a blue glass bottle.

Suggestions: Visualize a calming blue light swirling around your throat.

Crystal: Blue lace agate, aquamarine.

6. Third Eye Chakra (Ajna)

Color: Indigo

Meaning: Intuition, insight, wisdom.

Healing with Color: Use deep indigo colors in your environment, meditate with amethyst or lapis lazuli, or imagine an indigo light illuminating your forehead.

Suggestions: Incorporate indigo-colored fabrics or visualizations during deep meditation.

Crystal: Amethyst, lapis lazuli.

7. Crown Chakra (Sahasrara)

Color: Violet or White

Meaning: Spiritual connection, enlightenment.

Healing with Color: Visualize violet or white light descending into your crown, wear violet clothing, or use selenite and clear quartz.

Suggestions: Meditate under soft, violet-colored lighting or gaze at the stars for spiritual inspiration.

Crystal: Clear quartz, selenite.

Ways to Use Color for Chakra Healing

1. Visualization: Imagine the chakra's color glowing brightly in its location, expanding with each breath.

2. Clothing and Accessories: Wear colors associated with the chakra you want to balance.

3. Light Therapy: Use colored lights or LED bulbs to bathe a room in the chakra's color.

4. Crystals and Stones: Use crystals of corresponding colors (e.g., red jasper for Root Chakra, amethyst for Crown Chakra).

5. Nature Connection: Surround yourself with natural elements in chakra-related colors (e.g., green fields for the Heart Chakra, blue skies for the Throat Chakra).

6. Art and Decor: Incorporate chakra colors into your surroundings through art, fabrics, or decorations.

7. Food and Diet: Eat foods of the corresponding colors (e.g., red apples for Root Chakra, orange carrots for Sacral Chakra).

Chakra Color Meditation

Sit comfortably in a quiet space with soft lighting or candles in chakra colors.

Focus on Each Chakra: Start at the Root Chakra and work your way up to the Crown Chakra.

Visualize Colors: Imagine a vibrant red at the base of your spine, shifting to orange, yellow, green, blue, indigo, and violet as you move upward.

Meaning of Colours:

White(comprises all the 7 colours): Spiritual

VIBGYOR

COOLING COLOURS:

1. Violet: Artistic, Inspired, Imaginative
2. Indigo: Intuitive, Thoughtful, Communicative
3. Blue: Kind, Honest, Nurturing

BRIDGING COLOUR BETWEEN WARM AND COOL COLOURS:

1. Green: Balanced, Loving, Harmonious

WARMING COLOURS:

1. Yellow: Confident, Generous
2. Orange: Creative, Expressive, Productive
3. Red: Grounded, Stable

CHAPTER XXXVI

CHAKRAS AND CRYSTALS

Crystal healing involves using gemstones and minerals for their energetic properties to balance and align the chakras or to address specific issues.

Crystals work by emitting specific vibrations that harmonize with the frequency of the chakras. By placing a crystal on or near the chakra, the energy of the stone is believed to amplify the energy flow and help clear blockages.

Chakras and crystal healing are fascinating topics, blending ancient spiritual practices and modern holistic healing.

1. Root Chakra (Muladhara) – Stability, grounding, survival - Red jasper, hematite.
2. Sacral Chakra (Svadhisthana) – Creativity, emotions, pleasure - Carnelian, moonstone.
3. Solar Plexus Chakra (Manipura) – Confidence, willpower, self-esteem - Citrine, tiger's eye.
4. Heart Chakra (Anahata) – Love, compassion, relationships - Rose quartz, green aventurine.
5. Throat Chakra (Vishuddha) – Communication, truth, self-expression - Blue lace agate, aquamarine.
6. Third Eye Chakra (Ajna) – Intuition, insight, wisdom - Amethyst, lapis lazuli.
7. Crown Chakra (Sahasrara) – Spiritual connection, enlightenment - Clear quartz, selenite.

Crystals are often placed on the body, worn as jewelry, or kept in spaces to promote healing and energetic flow.

CHAPTER XXXVII

CHAKRAS AND DRESSING

Clothing not only serves as a way to cover and protect the body, but it also has the power to influence our energy, mood, and overall well-being. The chakra system, which governs our physical, emotional, and spiritual energies, can be positively or negatively affected by the clothes we wear. When we dress in alignment with the energy of the chakras, we can enhance balance, confidence, and vitality.

Our clothing choices can have a powerful effect on the way we feel, think, and interact with the world. By wearing colors, fabrics, and styles that correspond to the energy of the chakras, we can enhance our personal well-being, align our energy, and create a sense of balance and harmony in our lives. The way we dress can be a conscious expression of our inner energy, helping us to feel more grounded, empowered, loved, and connected to our higher self.

Each chakra has specific colors, fabrics, and styles of clothing that can resonate with its energy and help us align with the qualities associated with that chakra. By intentionally choosing clothing based on the energy centers, we can enhance self-expression, emotional health, and spiritual connection.

1. Root Chakra (Muladhara): Stability, Grounding, and Security

The Root Chakra, located at the base of the spine, governs our sense of security, grounding, and survival. Clothing that offers a sense of stability, comfort, and connection to the Earth is ideal for balancing this chakra.

Colors:

Red: Represents strength, vitality, and stability.

Earthy tones: Brown, black, dark green, and deep gray.

Fabrics:

Natural fibers such as cotton, linen, wool, or leather.

Fabrics that are heavy or solid, such as denim or thick wool, can also create a grounded feeling.

Styles:

Clothing that is well-fitted and supportive, such as boots, heavy coats, or sturdy pants.

Simple, practical clothing that makes you feel secure and comfortable.

How It Helps:

Wearing clothing in grounding colors and materials can help you feel more secure, stable, and connected to your physical body. Red tones stimulate energy and vitality, which can improve your overall sense of safety and survival.

2. Sacral Chakra (Svadhisthana): Creativity, Emotion, and Pleasure

The Sacral Chakra is associated with emotions, creativity, and sensuality. Clothing that is fluid, sensual, and inviting helps to balance this chakra and enhance emotional expression.

Colors:

Orange: Represents creativity, joy, and pleasure.

Peach, coral, and warm yellow tones.

Fabrics:

Soft, flowing fabrics like silk, satin, or cotton.

Clothes that allow freedom of movement and feel comfortable against the skin.

Styles:

Clothes with soft curves, flowing skirts, or loose tops.

Clothing that encourages movement, like dancewear or loose-fitting garments that embrace the body's fluid energy.

How It Helps:

Wearing orange or peach colors encourages emotional expression, creativity, and pleasure. The softness and flow of fabrics allow for free movement, enhancing sensuality and emotional release. Wearing clothing that feels good on your skin supports emotional well-being and enhances self-love.

3. Solar Plexus Chakra (Manipura): Confidence, Power, and Willpower

The Solar Plexus Chakra is linked to personal power, confidence, and self-esteem. Clothing that is bold, empowering, and bright can activate the energy of this chakra and encourage self-expression.

Colors:

Yellow: Represents strength, clarity, and power.

Gold: Symbolizes abundance, confidence, and success.

Fabrics:

Fabrics that are stiff, structured, and assertive such as denim, linen, or leather.

Bright fabrics that are eye-catching and inspire action, like silk, satin, or cotton in vibrant shades.

Styles:

Tailored clothing, such as jackets, blazers, or structured shirts that show a sense of power and confidence.

Accessories like bold jewelry, sunglasses, or items that draw attention to the solar plexus area (like belts or waistbands) can help emphasize this area.

How It Helps:

Wearing yellow, gold, or other bright colors can stimulate the Solar Plexus, boosting personal confidence and willpower. Structured clothing that fits well and creates a confident silhouette supports feelings of self-assurance and empowerment.

4. Heart Chakra (Anahata): Love, Compassion, and Emotional Healing

The Heart Chakra is associated with love, compassion, and emotional balance. Clothing that is soft, comforting, and heart-centered can help open and balance the energy of the heart.

Colors:

Green: Represents healing, growth, and unconditional love.

Pink: Symbolizes compassion, kindness, and nurturing.

Fabrics:

Soft, comfortable fabrics like cotton, wool, or flannel.

Natural fibers that promote comfort and warmth, like fleece or jersey.

Styles:

Loose-fitting garments like sweaters, cardigans, or coats that provide a sense of comfort and openness.

Layered clothing that allows freedom and emotional space for connection.

How It Helps:

Wearing green or pink clothing promotes emotional healing, love, and compassion. Soft, comfortable fabrics allow for a gentle embrace of the body, encouraging the flow of unconditional love and openness to both giving and receiving affection.

5. Throat Chakra (Vishuddha): Communication, Expression, and Truth

The Throat Chakra governs communication and self-expression. Clothing that is cooling, comforting, and open can help balance this chakra and encourage clear communication.

Colors:

Blue: Represents communication, truth, and clarity.

Turquoise and light blue.

Fabrics:

Light, breathable fabrics such as cotton, silk, or linen.

Fabrics that are cooling and breathable, especially around the neck area.

Styles:

Open-necked clothing, such as v-neck tops, loose scarves, or collarless shirts to free up the throat.

Accessories like necklaces or scarves that draw attention to the throat and enhance vocal expression.

How It Helps:

Wearing blue clothing supports clear communication and helps to open the Throat Chakra. Light fabrics around the neck area allow for a better flow of energy and support self-expression through speech and creativity. Clothes with open necklines give room for the throat to relax and speak freely.

6. Third Eye Chakra (Ajna): Intuition, Clarity, and Wisdom

The Third Eye Chakra governs intuition, wisdom, and mental clarity. Clothing that is deep, thoughtful, and mystical can help activate the energy of this chakra.

Colors:

Indigo: Represents insight, vision, and intuition.

Purple: Associated with higher consciousness and spiritual wisdom.

Fabrics:

Soft fabrics like velvet, silk, and cotton encourage introspection and quiet reflection.

Fabrics with a shimmering or mystical quality that inspire spiritual awareness.

Styles:

Clothing with deep tones such as indigo or purple in draped, flowing designs.

Items that inspire a sense of deep thought and wisdom, like robes or mystical accessories such as headbands or hats.

How It Helps:

Wearing indigo or purple clothing helps stimulate the Third Eye, enhancing intuition and mental clarity. Soft, flowing fabrics encourage introspection and connect us to higher wisdom, fostering deeper insight and spiritual awakening.

7. Crown Chakra (Sahasrara): Spirituality, Enlightenment, and Connection

The Crown Chakra is the center of spiritual connection, enlightenment, and higher consciousness. Clothing that is pure, light, and elevating can support the energy of this chakra.

Colors:

White: Represents purity, peace, and divine connection.

Violet and lavender: Symbolize higher consciousness and enlightenment.

Fabrics:

Light, ethereal fabrics like silk, linen, or organza(a thin, plain weave, sheer fabric traditionally made from silk).

White or light-colored fabrics that support purity and openness.

Styles:

Simple, clean styles that do not distract from the deeper connection to the divine.

Flowing garments, such as robes or dresses, that allow freedom of movement and connection to higher energies.

How It Helps:

Wearing white or violet clothing helps promote spiritual clarity and connection with higher consciousness. Light fabrics encourage openness and support the Crown Chakra's role in spiritual awakening, facilitating a deeper connection to the universe.

CHAPTER XXXVIII

CHAKRAS AND EFT

Emotional Freedom Techniques (EFT), often referred to as "tapping," is a form of energy psychology that combines aspects of cognitive therapy, exposure therapy, and acupressure. EFT involves tapping on specific meridian points on the body while focusing on emotional issues or physical discomfort. The theory behind EFT is that emotional blockages or trauma can disrupt the flow of energy in the body, leading to physical and emotional imbalances. By tapping on meridian points, EFT helps to restore balance and harmony to the body's energy system, including the chakras.

Chakras are energy centers within the body that regulate the flow of life force energy (prana, chi, etc.). When a chakra is blocked or imbalanced, it can manifest as physical illness, emotional distress, or spiritual stagnation. EFT can be an effective tool for clearing blockages in the chakras, releasing emotional trauma, and promoting energy flow, leading to overall healing and emotional freedom.

EFT is a powerful tool for healing the chakras, as it helps clear emotional blockages and restores energy flow. By using tapping techniques on specific meridian points and focusing on the emotional issues related to each chakra, you can release negative emotions, shift limiting beliefs, and promote balance and healing in your energy system. Whether used alone or in conjunction with other chakra-balancing practices, EFT can enhance your journey toward emotional freedom, personal empowerment, and spiritual growth.

How EFT Works with Chakras:

EFT works by addressing the emotional root causes of imbalances in the chakras. The tapping sequence targets specific meridian points that correspond to the body's energy pathways. These meridians are connected to the chakras, and by stimulating them, EFT can help clear blockages in the chakras and restore balance. EFT can help bring emotional awareness to issues stored in the chakras, such as fear, anger, shame, or guilt, and allow for emotional release and healing.

Each chakra is associated with specific emotions, beliefs, and experiences. By addressing these through tapping and focusing on the chakra-related issues, EFT can help release stored emotional energy, restore energetic flow, and bring healing to each chakra.

By focusing on positive affirmations during the tapping process, you can reprogram your subconscious mind, changing limiting beliefs that prevent chakra healing and personal growth.

EFT and the Seven Chakras:

1. Root Chakra (Muladhara) – Stability, Security, Grounding

Emotional Imbalances: Fear, insecurity, financial stress, survival anxiety.

EFT Focus: Tapping on the Root Chakra while focusing on fears of instability or feeling ungrounded. Affirmations might include "Even though I feel unsafe or insecure, I choose to feel grounded and supported."

Key Areas for Tapping: Base of the spine, lower back, and knees (which correspond to the Root Chakra).

2. Sacral Chakra (Svadhisthana) – Creativity, Emotions, Sexuality

Emotional Imbalances: Guilt, shame, emotional repression, sexual dysfunction.

EFT Focus: Tapping on the Sacral Chakra while acknowledging emotional wounds related to relationships, creativity, or sexuality. Affirmations might include "Even though I feel disconnected from my creativity or my emotional needs, I choose to embrace my emotions and feel safe expressing myself."

Key Areas for Tapping: Lower abdomen, pelvis, hips (connected to the Sacral Chakra).

3, Solar Plexus Chakra (Manipura) – Personal Power, Confidence, Willpower

Emotional Imbalances: Low self-esteem, lack of confidence, anger, frustration.

EFT Focus: Tapping on the Solar Plexus while addressing feelings of powerlessness, fear of failure, or self-judgment. Affirmations might include "Even though I doubt my strength and power, I choose to step into my confidence and trust in myself."

Key Areas for Tapping: Upper abdomen, solar plexus area, diaphragm.

4. Heart Chakra (Anahata) – Love, Compassion, Forgiveness

Emotional Imbalances: Grief, heartbreak, lack of self-love, emotional isolation.

EFT Focus: Tapping on the Heart Chakra while focusing on emotional wounds related to love, relationships, and forgiveness. Affirmations might include "Even though I have been hurt in the past, I choose to open my heart and allow love and compassion to flow."

Key Areas for Tapping: Center of the chest, upper back, and shoulder blades (related to the Heart Chakra).

5. Throat Chakra (Vishuddha) – Communication, Expression, Truth

Emotional Imbalances: Difficulty speaking up, fear of judgment, suppression of truth.

EFT Focus: Tapping on the Throat Chakra while addressing issues related to self-expression, fear of speaking your truth, or difficulty being heard. Affirmations might include "Even though I fear speaking my truth, I choose to express myself clearly and confidently."

Key Areas for Tapping: Throat, jaw, and neck.

6. Third Eye Chakra (Ajna) – Intuition, Insight, Clarity

Emotional Imbalances: Lack of clarity, feeling disconnected from intuition, confusion.

EFT Focus: Tapping on the Third Eye Chakra while addressing mental blockages, confusion, or fear of trusting intuition. Affirmations might include "Even though I am uncertain about my intuition, I choose to trust my inner wisdom and embrace clarity."

Key Areas for Tapping: Between the eyebrows (center of the forehead).

7. Crown Chakra (Sahasrara) – Spiritual Connection, Enlightenment, Oneness

Emotional Imbalances: Feeling disconnected from spirit, lack of purpose, spiritual confusion.

EFT Focus: Tapping on the Crown Chakra while addressing feelings of spiritual disconnection, lack of higher purpose, or difficulty accessing divine guidance. Affirmations might include "Even though I feel disconnected from my spiritual self, I choose to open to divine wisdom and universal connection."

Key Areas for Tapping: Top of the head.

NOTE: This method requires professional help, not recommended for self-healing.

CHAPTER XXXIX

CHAKRAS AND ENERGY BODIES

The concept of subtle bodies refers to the layers or energetic fields that exist around and within the physical body, each corresponding to different aspects of our consciousness and being. In many spiritual traditions, particularly those influenced by Eastern philosophies like Yoga and Ayurveda, the subtle bodies are seen as integral to understanding how our energy interacts with the physical, emotional, mental, and spiritual realms.

Each of the seven chakras is intimately connected with the subtle bodies that influence our physical, emotional, mental, and spiritual well-being. By understanding how these chakras interact with the subtle bodies, we can develop a deeper awareness of our energy system, allowing us to heal and balance the different layers of our being.

Overview of the Subtle Bodies

Each body is linked to a different level of consciousness and chakra:

1. **Physical Body (Annamaya Kosha)**: The dense, tangible body that is made up of matter and is what we typically think of when considering physical health.
2. **Energy Body (Pranamaya Kosha):** The field of life force energy (prana) that surrounds and permeates the physical body. It governs vitality, breath, and movement.
3. **Mental Body (Manomaya Kosha):** The body of thought and emotion, responsible for mental processes and emotional states.
4. **Wisdom Body (Vijnanamaya Kosha):** The body of higher knowledge, intellect, and discernment. It represents the aspect of consciousness that seeks truth and clarity.
5. **Bliss Body (Anandamaya Kosha):** The innermost body, representing pure bliss, joy, and connection with the divine. It is

associated with deep spiritual experiences and enlightenment.

1. Root Chakra (Muladhara) – Physical Body and Energy Body

Physical Body: The root chakra is directly connected to the physical body, influencing the basic physical functions related to survival, stability, and security. It governs the spine, legs, feet, and the excretory system.

Energy Body: The root chakra is also connected to the energy body (Pranamaya Kosha), as it provides the foundation for the flow of prana throughout the body. When this chakra is balanced, it helps stabilize the energy system, ensuring vitality and proper circulation of energy.

Imbalances in the Root Chakra: Fear, insecurity, anxiety, and a sense of being disconnected from the physical world. These can lead to health issues such as fatigue, lower back pain, and digestive problems.

Healing the Root Chakra: Grounding exercises, meditation, and physical practices such as yoga help to establish stability and balance in the root chakra, allowing prana to flow freely.

2. Sacral Chakra (Svadhisthana) – Energy Body and Mental Body

Energy Body: The sacral chakra is tied to the energy body as it regulates the flow of creative energy and life force. It governs the lower abdomen, pelvis, and reproductive organs, influencing creativity, sexuality, and emotional well-being.

Mental Body: This chakra is also linked to the mental body, influencing emotional expression, creativity, and the way emotions are processed mentally. When balanced, the sacral chakra promotes emotional flexibility and healthy relationships.

Imbalances in the Sacral Chakra: Blockages can lead to emotional instability, issues with self-worth, and lack of creativity. On the physical level, it can manifest as reproductive issues, lower back problems, or kidney issues.

Healing the Sacral Chakra: Engaging in creative expression (art, dance, writing), emotional healing, and practices that connect you to your sensual and emotional experiences can restore balance in this chakra.

3. Solar Plexus Chakra (Manipura) – Mental Body and Wisdom Body

Mental Body: The solar plexus chakra governs the mental body, influencing self-esteem, willpower, and the ability to make decisions. It is the center of mental clarity and intellectual processing, impacting how we approach challenges and take control of our lives.

Wisdom Body: This chakra also corresponds to the wisdom body, as it plays a key role in discernment and critical thinking. The solar plexus helps us take action based on self-confidence and inner clarity, which are necessary for understanding our purpose in life.

Imbalances in the Solar Plexus Chakra: Low self-esteem, indecisiveness, lack of confidence, and overwhelm. Physical symptoms can include digestive issues, liver problems, and adrenal fatigue.

Healing the Solar Plexus Chakra: To restore balance, focus on confidence-building activities, practices like assertiveness training, and self-care routines that empower your sense of personal strength.

4. Heart Chakra (Anahata) – Mental Body and Bliss Body

Mental Body: The heart chakra influences how we relate to others emotionally and mentally. It governs our ability to connect with empathy, love, and compassion, and forms the bridge between the lower and upper chakras.

Bliss Body: The heart chakra is also linked to the bliss body, as it is the seat of unconditional love and joy. When balanced, it allows a person to experience true peace, connection, and love, offering deep spiritual fulfillment.

Imbalances in the Heart Chakra: A blocked heart chakra can lead to emotional numbness, difficulty in forming relationships, feelings of loneliness, or being emotionally closed off. It can also manifest physically as respiratory problems, cardiovascular issues, or chest pain.

Healing the Heart Chakra: Practices of forgiveness, compassion, and unconditional love toward oneself and others can help clear blockages. Heart-centered meditation and physical activities such as heart-opening yoga poses can be beneficial.

5. Throat Chakra (Vishuddha) – Energy Body and Mental Body

Energy Body: The throat chakra influences the energy body in terms of communication and expression. It governs the throat, vocal cords, and the respiratory system, playing a significant role in how we express ourselves energetically.

Mental Body: This chakra also governs the mental body's thoughts and words, affecting how we articulate our inner truth and interact with the world verbally. The throat chakra is essential for clear communication and honesty.

Imbalances in the Throat Chakra: A blocked throat chakra can cause feelings of powerlessness, difficulty expressing one's thoughts or desires, or a tendency to hold back opinions. Physical manifestations might include sore throats, neck pain, or thyroid imbalances.

Healing the Throat Chakra: Practices like singing, writing, and engaging in honest self-expression can help heal this chakra. Journaling and speaking your truth in safe environments also contribute to its balance.

6. Third Eye Chakra (Ajna) – Wisdom Body and Bliss Body

Wisdom Body: The third eye chakra connects deeply with the wisdom body, representing intuition, clarity, and insight. It governs the mind's ability to perceive truth and access higher knowledge. This chakra helps us navigate the world with clear discernment.

Bliss Body: The third eye chakra also relates to the bliss body, as it provides access to the deeper spiritual realm and the experience of oneness with the universe. It is the gateway to understanding higher consciousness and spiritual truths.

Imbalances in the Third Eye Chakra: Blockages can result in a lack of clarity, confusion, and a weakened ability to trust your intuition. This can lead to poor decision-making and feelings of disconnection from one's purpose. Physical issues may include headaches, eye strain, or sinus problems.

Healing the Third Eye Chakra: Engage in meditation, visualization exercises, and practices that help develop intuitive awareness. Journaling dreams, focusing on inner guidance, and trusting your inner vision can help balance this chakra.

7. Crown Chakra (Sahasrara) – Bliss Body

Bliss Body: The crown chakra is directly connected to the bliss body, representing pure spiritual consciousness and connection to the divine or universal energy. It governs the mind's ability to transcend ego and experience unity with the cosmos.

Spiritual Connection: The crown chakra represents the final layer of subtle energy, guiding us toward a higher state of consciousness and spiritual enlightenment.

Imbalances in the Crown Chakra: A blocked crown chakra can lead to feelings of spiritual disconnection, meaninglessness, and a lack of purpose. Physical symptoms may include headaches or issues with the nervous system.

Healing the Crown Chakra: Engage in spiritual practices, like meditation, prayer, or mindfulness. Trusting in the greater flow of life and connecting to higher wisdom can help balance this chakra and deepen the sense of spiritual connection.

CHAPTER XL

CHAKRAS AND ENERGY

Energy healing is a holistic therapeutic approach that aims to balance the body's energy systems, including the chakras, to promote physical, emotional, and spiritual well-being. Chakras, as energy centers in the body, are believed to govern the flow of life force or "chi" (also known as prana, qi, or energy). When this energy is blocked, misaligned, or imbalanced, it can lead to physical ailments, emotional distress, and a general sense of disconnection from oneself. Energy healing practices work to remove blockages, restore balance, and allow energy to flow freely through the chakras, promoting overall health.

Energy healing methods can help individuals identify, address, and release blockages or imbalances in the chakra system, facilitating self-healing and enhancing vitality.

Energy healing offers a powerful tool for restoring balance and alignment to the chakra system. Through practices like reiki or pranic healing, crystal healing, sound therapy, and more, individuals can clear blockages, release stagnant energy, and promote holistic healing. By addressing the energetic imbalances in the chakras

Common Forms of Energy Healing Used for Chakra Balancing:

Reiki: Reiki is a Japanese energy healing modality that involves the practitioner channeling healing energy into the patient through their hands. The goal of Reiki is to remove blockages in the chakras and restore the flow of life force energy throughout the body. Reiki practitioners work with the energy fields around the body, known as the aura, and focus on specific chakras to bring them back into balance. Reiki is often deeply relaxing and can result in emotional release and physical healing.

How it Works with Chakras: The Reiki practitioner will either lightly touch or hover their hands over specific chakras to direct healing energy. For example, if someone is experiencing emotional blockages in the Heart Chakra, the practitioner will focus on healing energy there, encouraging emotional healing, compassion, and balance.

Crystal Healing: Crystal healing involves the use of gemstones and crystals to align and balance the chakra system. Each chakra is associated with specific crystals that resonate with the energy of that chakra. For example, amethyst is often used for the Third Eye Chakra, while rose quartz is associated with the Heart Chakra. The stones are placed on or near the body to help draw out negative energy and replace it with positive, healing energy.

How it Works with Chakras: Crystals work by emitting specific vibrations that harmonize with the frequency of the chakras. By placing a crystal on or near the chakra, the energy of the stone is believed to amplify the energy flow and help clear blockages. For instance, placing a red jasper crystal on the Root Chakra can promote grounding, while clear quartz placed on the Crown Chakra can enhance spiritual connection.

Sound Healing (Sound Therapy): Sound healing involves the use of sound frequencies to heal the body, mind, and spirit. Certain sound frequencies resonate with the vibrations of the chakras, helping to restore balance and harmony. Techniques such as singing bowls, tuning forks, chanting, and drumming are commonly used in sound healing practices to address chakra imbalances.

How it Works with Chakras: Each chakra has its own frequency and vibrational energy. For example, the root chakra resonates with a low, grounding sound, while the Third Eye Chakra has a higher frequency. By using sound that matches the frequency of each chakra, practitioners can help clear blockages and restore energetic balance. Tibetan singing bowls or crystal bowls tuned to the specific frequencies of the chakras are often used to facilitate this healing.

Pranic Healing: Pranic healing is an energy healing technique that works with the body's energy field to remove blockages and balance the chakras. It involves the use of the hands to scan and clear the energy body, focusing on specific chakras. A trained Pranic healers can feel areas of imbalance and then use techniques such as sweeping or energizing to restore balance.

How it Works with Chakras: Pranic healers focus on the energy body and the chakras, identifying where energy is stagnant or deficient. Through a combination of scanning, cleansing, and energizing, they remove blockages and promote healing. For example, if the Solar Plexus Chakra is blocked, the healer may focus on clearing negative energy and infusing the chakra with healing energy to restore confidence and personal power.

Acupuncture and Acupressure: Acupuncture is a traditional Chinese medicine practice that involves inserting thin needles into specific points on the body to restore the flow of energy. Acupressure, on the other hand, uses pressure applied to these points. These practices aim to clear blockages and ensure the free flow of energy (Qi) throughout the body, including through the chakras.

How it Works with Chakras: Certain acupuncture or acupressure points correspond to the chakras. For example, points along the spine are commonly associated with the Root Chakra, while points on the forehead or around the eyes may be connected to the Third Eye Chakra. By stimulating these points, energy blockages in the chakras can be cleared, and the overall energy flow is enhanced.

Chakras and Energy Healing Techniques for Each Chakra:

1. Root Chakra (Muladhara) – Stability and Grounding: Energy healing techniques for the Root Chakra focus on grounding and restoring feelings of safety and security. Practices like Reiki or crystal healing using grounding stones such as hematite or red jasper are helpful in re-establishing balance.

Healing Techniques: Grounding exercises, use of red stones like garnet or ruby, and sound healing using low-pitched sounds or drumming.

2. Sacral Chakra (Svadhisthana) – Emotions and Creativity: Energy healing for the Sacral Chakra addresses emotional blockages and creative expression. Orange crystals like carnelian or orange calcite, or essential oils such as sandalwood, can be used to open and balance this chakra.

Healing Techniques: Use of fluid movements (e.g., dancing or tai chi), reiki or pranic healing, and crystals like carnelian or moonstone.

3. Solar Plexus Chakra (Manipura) – Personal Power and Confidence: The Solar Plexus Chakra governs self-esteem, personal power, and willpower. Energy healing techniques focus on boosting confidence and clearing any emotional blockages related to self-worth. Citrine, tiger's eye, and yellow aventurine are commonly used crystals for this chakra.

Healing Techniques: Breathwork, reiki or pranic healing,, use of yellow crystals like citrine or amber, and guided visualizations focusing on personal empowerment.

4. Heart Chakra (Anahata) – Love and Compassion: Energy healing for the Heart Chakra involves releasing past pain, grief, and heartbreak while promoting love, compassion, and forgiveness. Rose quartz, green aventurine, and emerald are healing stones for the Heart Chakra.

Healing Techniques: Heart-centered meditations, reiki or pranic healing, using rose quartz or jade crystals, and sound healing with heart-opening frequencies (e.g., singing bowls tuned to the Heart Chakra).

5. Throat Chakra (Vishuddha) – Communication and Expression: Energy healing for the Throat Chakra focuses on clearing blockages related to self-expression, communication, and speaking one's truth. Crystals such as aquamarine, lapis lazuli, or turquoise are commonly used to heal this chakra.

Healing Techniques: Chanting, singing, sound healing with Tibetan singing bowls, reiki or pranic healing, and blue crystals like turquoise or sodalite.

6. Third Eye Chakra (Ajna) – Intuition and Clarity: Healing for the Third Eye Chakra involves clearing mental fog, enhancing intuition, and promoting spiritual insight. Amethyst, lapis lazuli, and clear quartz are powerful stones for this chakra.

Healing Techniques: Meditation, mindfulness, reiki or pranic healing, sound healing with high-frequency tones, and the use of amethyst or sodalite crystals(rich blue in colour).

7. Crown Chakra (Sahasrara) – Spiritual Connection and Enlightenment: The Crown Chakra represents spiritual connection and enlightenment. Energy healing for this chakra focuses on releasing spiritual blockages, enhancing consciousness, and aligning with higher wisdom. Clear quartz, selenite, and diamond are commonly used crystals for this chakra.

Healing Techniques: Meditation, guided visualization, reiki or pranic healing, and sound healing with high-pitched tones or chanting to stimulate higher consciousness.

Integrating Energy Healing and Chakra Work:

Integrating energy healing with chakra work can significantly enhance the benefits of both practices. For example, someone may undergo reiki or pranic healing to release blockages in the Heart Chakra while simultaneously using affirmations to promote self-love and compassion. Combining energy healing modalities like crystal healing, and sound therapy, with chakra balancing techniques can accelerate the healing process and support long-term well-being.

NOTE: These methods require professional help, not recommended for self-healing.

CHAPTER XLI

CHAKRAS AND FOOD

Chakras and food are deeply interconnected, as the energy and nutrients from food can help balance and energize each chakra. By choosing specific foods that correspond to the vibrational energy and color of each chakra, you can support their alignment and overall wellbeing.

Food is more than just fuel for the body; it has a profound impact on our energy, emotions, and consciousness. In the same way that the chakra system governs different aspects of our well-being, the foods we eat can influence and balance our energy centers.

By understanding how different foods align with the chakras, we can make dietary choices that support not only physical health but also emotional, mental, and spiritual balance.

By choosing foods that support each chakra, you can align your physical body, emotions, and spirit, allowing for a balanced and harmonious flow of energy. The practice of eating with chakra awareness is a holistic approach that fosters well-being on all levels.

Each chakra has specific dietary needs and preferences, which help to balance energy, enhance vitality, and align us with our higher purpose.

Foods that are light and pure help maintain the body's vibrational frequency and support spiritual connection. They promote an open mind, facilitating deep meditation and spiritual experiences that align with the higher self.

1. Root Chakra (Muladhara): Nourishing Stability and Grounding

The Root Chakra is connected to our survival instincts, stability, and grounding. It governs our connection to the Earth and our sense of safety. Foods that are rooted, hearty, and grounding help to strengthen this chakra. Root vegetables, proteins, and foods that provide long-lasting energy can support a balanced Root Chakra.

Foods for the Root Chakra:

Associated Foods: Foods that grow underground or are red in color.

Root Vegetables: Carrots, potatoes, beets, turnips, sweet potatoes.

Proteins: Red meats, beans, lentils, nuts, and seeds.

Grains: Brown rice, quinoa, oats, whole wheat.

Spices: Garlic, ginger, cinnamon (warming and grounding).

Hydration: Water, herbal teas like ginger or root-based teas.

Tip: Choose hearty, earthy meals to feel grounded and nourished.

How They Help:

These foods help establish a sense of physical stability, increase energy, and provide nourishment for the body, reinforcing feelings of security. Root vegetables, in particular, represent the grounding energy of the Earth.

2. Sacral Chakra (Svadhisthana): Cultivating Creativity and Emotional Flow

The Sacral Chakra governs our creativity, emotions, and desires. It thrives on the flow of energy and is nourished by foods that stimulate our senses and encourage pleasure and abundance. Foods that are sweet, hydrating, and moist align with the Sacral Chakra.

Foods for the Sacral Chakra:

Sweet Fruits: Oranges, mangoes, strawberries, melons, and peaches.

Nuts and Seeds: Almonds, walnuts, sunflower seeds.

Oily Foods: Healthy oils like olive oil, coconut oil, avocado.

Dairy: Milk, yogurt, and cheese (for those who tolerate dairy).

Spices: Cinnamon, vanilla, and cardamom.

Tip: Include foods that are rich in healthy fats, like nuts and seeds, to support emotional balance and creative energy.

How They Help:

Sweet and hydrating foods help to activate the energy of this chakra, supporting emotional well-being and creativity. These foods enhance sensuality and help to open the flow of emotions, fostering a sense of inner pleasure and fulfillment.

3. Solar Plexus Chakra (Manipura): Boosting Confidence and Personal Power

The Solar Plexus Chakra is the seat of personal power, confidence, and willpower. Foods that energize, strengthen, and support digestion help to activate and balance this chakra. These foods often have a yellow color, representing the Sun's energy.

Foods for the Solar Plexus Chakra:

Yellow Foods: Bananas, corn, yellow peppers, yellow squash.

Whole Grains: Oats, barley, millet.

Spices: Turmeric, ginger, and mustard.

Legumes: Chickpeas, lentils, and peas.

Proteins: Eggs, lean meats, and tofu.

Tip: Opt for foods that are easy to digest and provide sustainable energy.

How They Help:

Yellow foods stimulate the digestive system and provide energy, aligning with the Solar Plexus' role in personal empowerment and mental clarity. These foods help to strengthen the body's internal fire, improving self-esteem and motivation.

4. Heart Chakra (Anahata): Nourishing Love and Compassion

The Heart Chakra is the center of love, compassion, and emotional healing. To balance this chakra, foods that are green, nourishing, and heart-healthy help to open the heart and promote feelings of love and connection.

Foods for the Heart Chakra:

Leafy Greens: Kale, spinach.

Fruits: Apples, pears, grapes, avocados.

Nuts and Seeds: Walnuts, flaxseeds, pumpkin seeds.

Herbs: Basil, oregano, thyme, and parsley.

Teas: Green tea, chamomile.

Tip: Incorporate foods rich in antioxidants and healthy fats to nourish the heart and promote emotional harmony.

How They Help:

Green foods are rich in vitamins and minerals that promote heart health and emotional healing. They help open the heart, encourage compassion, and foster deep emotional connections with others. The heart is nourished both physically and energetically through these plant-based foods.

5. Throat Chakra (Vishuddha): Enhancing Communication and Self-Expression

The Throat Chakra is responsible for clear communication, self-expression, and truth. Foods that are blue or cooling, which soothe and support the throat, are ideal for this chakra. They should also be light and help to clear blockages in the throat area.

Foods for the Throat Chakra:

Blue Foods: Blueberries, blackberries, grapes, and plums.

Cooling Foods: Cucumbers, melons, coconut water, and mint.

Herbal Teas: Peppermint, chamomile, and licorice root (soothing for the throat).

Clear Liquids: Water, fresh juices, and teas to hydrate and clear the throat.

Tip: Stay hydrated with water and herbal teas to support clear communication and throat health.

How They Help:

Cooling foods and liquids help to calm and soothe the throat, promoting clear speech and expression. Blue foods are naturally calming and can help facilitate better communication and the expression of personal truth.

6. Third Eye Chakra (Ajna): Enhancing Intuition and Wisdom

The Third Eye Chakra is the center of intuition, wisdom, and insight. Foods that stimulate the brain, promote clarity, and encourage higher thinking are beneficial for this chakra. Foods rich in antioxidants and those that support mental clarity are key.

Foods for the Third Eye Chakra:

Purple Foods: Eggplant, purple grapes, purple cabbage, and plums.

Leafy Greens: Kale, spinach, and chard (also good for clarity).

Nuts and Seeds: Walnuts (good for brain function), flaxseeds, chia seeds.

Herbs: Sage, rosemary (good for mental clarity and focus).

Tip: Choose foods that support brain health, like walnuts, chia seeds, and omega-3-rich options.

How They Help:

Purple and dark-colored foods are linked with the Third Eye Chakra and support mental clarity, focus, and spiritual insight. These foods help stimulate the brain and promote the development of intuitive abilities.

7. Crown Chakra (Sahasrara): Nourishing Spiritual Connection

The Crown Chakra is the center of spiritual connection and enlightenment. It is nourished by foods that promote purity and elevate consciousness. These foods are light, clean, and support the body's spiritual and energetic systems.

Foods for the Crown Chakra:

Light, Pure Foods: Fresh fruits and vegetables, herbal teas, and water.

Fasting: Occasional fasting or consuming light foods helps open the Crown Chakra by promoting spiritual clarity and connection.

Whole Foods: Organic foods, especially those rich in nutrients and grown without chemicals.

Tip: Incorporate fasting or simple diets occasionally to enhance spiritual clarity.

General Tips for Chakra Food Healing

1. Eat the Rainbow: Including a variety of colorful fruits and vegetables ensures that all chakras receive energy.
2. Mindful Eating: Take time to savor each bite, focusing on the energy and nourishment the food provides.
3. Natural and Whole Foods: Avoid processed foods and opt for fresh, organic ingredients to maintain the purity of energy.
4. Balance: Combine physical, emotional, and spiritual practices with your diet for holistic chakra alignment.

CHAPTER XLII

CHAKRAS AND HYPNOTHERAPY

Hypnotherapy is a powerful tool for accessing the subconscious mind, where many of our beliefs, emotions, and blockages reside. The practice can be used to identify and address issues related to the chakras, facilitating healing and balance. By working with the chakra system through hypnotherapy, you can unlock deeper layers of emotional and spiritual blockages, clear negative patterns, and promote healing on a profound level.

How Hypnotherapy Can Facilitate Chakra Healing:

Hypnotherapy involves entering a deep state of relaxation (a trance-like state), where the conscious mind becomes quiet, and the subconscious mind becomes more accessible. In this state, you can work directly with the chakras, identifying and healing issues that may be preventing them from functioning optimally.

Using Hypnotherapy to Clear Blockages in Each Chakra:

1. Root Chakra (Muladhara) and Hypnotherapy

Focus: Grounding, Safety, Security, and Stability

The Root Chakra is foundational to feelings of safety and security in the world. If you've experienced trauma, fear, or instability, these feelings may be stored in this chakra.

Hypnotherapy Process: In a hypnotherapy session for Root Chakra healing, the therapist may guide you to recall past experiences related to fear, insecurity, or instability. The goal is to uncover limiting beliefs or traumatic events that have affected your sense of security. Techniques like regression (going back to childhood or earlier experiences) or suggestion therapy can be used to reframe those beliefs and replace them with empowering ones.

Potential Outcomes: After addressing Root Chakra blockages through hypnotherapy, clients often experience a renewed sense of confidence, stability, and grounding in their daily lives. They may feel more connected to their bodies and the present moment, fostering an increased sense of security.

2. Sacral Chakra (Svadhisthana) and Hypnotherapy

Focus: Emotions, Creativity, Sensuality, and Pleasure

The Sacral Chakra is related to emotional expression, creativity, and relationships. Blockages here may arise from emotional trauma, guilt, or fear of expressing desires.

Hypnotherapy Process: Hypnotherapy can help uncover suppressed emotions, negative beliefs about pleasure or creativity, or trauma related to relationships. Through regression techniques, the therapist may guide you to uncover past experiences of shame, guilt, or emotional suppression. Suggestions can be provided to release negative emotions and open the flow of creative and emotional energy.

Potential Outcomes: After hypnotherapy for the Sacral Chakra, clients may feel more comfortable expressing their emotions and desires without guilt or shame. Creativity may flow more freely, and they may experience greater pleasure in their relationships and personal life.

3. Solar Plexus Chakra (Manipura) and Hypnotherapy

Focus: Personal Power, Confidence, Self-Worth, and Willpower

The Solar Plexus Chakra governs our sense of personal power, self-esteem, and confidence. Blockages in this chakra often stem from feelings of powerlessness, low self-worth, or a lack of confidence.

Hypnotherapy Process: A hypnotherapist may guide you into a deeply relaxed state and then use suggestion therapy to enhance self-esteem, confidence, and personal power. Through hypnotherapy, you can revisit situations where you felt disempowered or where you lacked confidence and reframe those experiences. Positive suggestions and affirmations are often used to encourage self-worth and empowerment.

Potential Outcomes: After hypnotherapy for the Solar Plexus Chakra, clients often report a stronger sense of personal power and greater confidence. They may feel more assertive, able to set boundaries, and pursue their goals with greater determination.

4. Heart Chakra (Anahata) and Hypnotherapy

Focus: Love, Compassion, and Emotional Healing

The Heart Chakra is the center of love and compassion, both for others and for yourself. If this chakra is blocked, it can result in emotional pain, difficulty in relationships, or a lack of self-love.

Hypnotherapy Process: Hypnotherapy can be used to uncover any past experiences of emotional pain, betrayal, or grief that are blocking the Heart Chakra. Through guided regression, the therapist may help you release past hurts, forgive others, and learn to cultivate self-love. Suggestions can be used to open the heart and promote compassion for yourself and others.

Potential Outcomes: Clients who undergo hypnotherapy for Heart Chakra healing often experience greater emotional freedom, the ability to forgive, and an increased sense of love for themselves and others. They may find themselves more open to giving and receiving love.

5. Throat Chakra (Vishuddha) and Hypnotherapy

Focus: Communication, Truth, and Self-Expression

The Throat Chakra is associated with verbal communication and the ability to speak your truth. Blockages here can result in difficulty expressing oneself, fear of speaking, or a tendency to suppress one's opinions.

Hypnotherapy Process: In a hypnotherapy session for Throat Chakra healing, the therapist may help you access past experiences where you felt unable to speak up or express your truth. The goal is to release any fears or limiting beliefs that may be holding you back from communicating openly. Suggestions may be given to enhance self-expression, confidence in speaking, and a deeper connection to your authentic voice.

Potential Outcomes: After hypnotherapy for the Throat Chakra, clients may feel more empowered to speak their truth and express themselves clearly. They may also experience a greater sense of ease in communication, both in personal and professional settings.

6. Third Eye Chakra (Ajna) and Hypnotherapy

Focus: Intuition, Insight, and Inner Wisdom
The Third Eye Chakra is connected to intuition and the ability to see beyond the material world. Blockages here may prevent you from trusting your inner guidance or seeing the bigger picture.

Hypnotherapy Process: Through hypnotherapy, clients can explore past experiences or beliefs that are preventing them from trusting their intuition or gaining clarity. Regression techniques can help uncover mental or emotional blockages that limit the ability to perceive deeper truths. The therapist may also use suggestion therapy to strengthen intuition and promote clarity of thought.

Potential Outcomes: After working on the Third Eye Chakra with hypnotherapy, clients may experience heightened intuition, a clearer understanding of their life purpose, and increased inner clarity. They may also develop a stronger sense of trust in their intuitive insights.

7. Crown Chakra (Sahasrara) and Hypnotherapy

Focus: Spiritual Connection, Enlightenment, and Higher Consciousness
The Crown Chakra connects us to the divine and the universal consciousness. Blockages in the Crown Chakra may manifest as feelings of disconnection from the spiritual realm or a lack of meaning in life.

Hypnotherapy Process: Hypnotherapy for Crown Chakra healing may focus on releasing any beliefs that create separation from the divine or higher consciousness. Through deep relaxation and guided visualization, the therapist may help you access spiritual wisdom, release attachments, and reconnect with the universal flow of energy.

Potential Outcomes: After hypnotherapy for the Crown Chakra, clients often report feeling more spiritually connected, experiencing a deeper sense of purpose, and gaining clarity about their spiritual path. They may also feel a greater sense of unity with the universe and a release from the ego's limitations.

Benefits of Combining Hypnotherapy with Chakra Healing:

Release of Deep-Seated Blockages: Hypnotherapy allows you to access the subconscious mind, where many of the blockages preventing chakra flow are stored.

Emotional Healing: Hypnotherapy facilitates emotional healing by helping you uncover and release repressed emotions that may be affecting your chakras.

Increased Awareness: Working with the chakras in a hypnotherapeutic setting can increase self-awareness and spiritual insight, allowing you to make more empowered choices in life.

Balanced Energy Flow: Through hypnotherapy, you can balance and harmonize the chakra system, leading to improved emotional, mental, and physical well-being.

NOTE: This method require professional help, not recommended for self-healing.

NOTE: Past Life Regression Therapy is similar to Hypno Therapy

CHAPTER XLIII

CHAKRAS AND MAGNET THERAPY

Magnet therapy, also known as magnetic field therapy, is an alternative healing practice that involves using magnets to influence the body's electromagnetic fields. The human body has an electromagnetic field, and magnetic fields can interact with the body's natural energy, promoting healing and restoring balance. Magnet therapy is sometimes used in conjunction with chakra healing, as it can help clear blockages and enhance the energy flow through the chakra system.

Magnet therapy can be a valuable tool in chakra healing by promoting the flow of energy, reducing blockages, and enhancing the body's natural healing abilities. It helps balance and activate the chakras, supporting overall well-being.

Each chakra has its own unique frequency and energy vibration, and using magnet therapy in alignment with the chakras can support their healing by increasing circulation, reducing inflammation, and balancing energy.

How Magnet Therapy Works with Chakras:

Magnetic fields can influence the body in several ways, including improving blood circulation, reducing pain and inflammation, and stimulating the production of endorphins. When applied to the chakra system, magnets can help to stimulate or balance the energy of each chakra, depending on the type of magnetic field used and the area being treated.

Magnet Therapy and the Chakras: An Overview

1. Root Chakra (Muladhara) and Magnet Therapy

Focus: Grounding, Security, Stability

The Root Chakra is associated with our sense of safety, stability, and connection to the Earth. A blocked or unbalanced Root Chakra may result in feelings of fear, insecurity, or being disconnected from the physical world.

Magnet Therapy for Root Chakra: Magnetic therapy can help ground and stabilize the Root Chakra. By placing magnets near the base of the spine (where the Root Chakra is located), you can stimulate energy flow, helping you feel more grounded and secure. Magnets with a north pole (negative) orientation are often used in this area to balance energy.

Benefits: Promotes a sense of physical grounding, reduces feelings of fear or anxiety, and supports a deep connection to the Earth.

2. Sacral Chakra (Svadhisthana) and Magnet Therapy

Focus: Emotions, Creativity, Pleasure

The Sacral Chakra is linked to emotions, creativity, and sensuality. A blocked Sacral Chakra may manifest as emotional instability, low libido, or creative blockages.

Magnet Therapy for Sacral Chakra: Placing magnets near the lower abdomen or pelvic region can stimulate the Sacral Chakra. Using magnets with a south pole (positive) orientation may encourage emotional flow, creativity, and vitality.

Benefits: Enhances creativity, encourages emotional release, and supports healthy sexual and reproductive energy.

3. Solar Plexus Chakra (Manipura) and Magnet Therapy

Focus: Personal Power, Confidence, Self-Worth

The Solar Plexus Chakra is the center of personal power, will, and confidence. If blocked, it can lead to feelings of low self-esteem, lack of direction, or difficulty asserting oneself.

Magnet Therapy for Solar Plexus Chakra: Magnets placed around the stomach or just above the navel (where the Solar Plexus is located) can help balance this chakra. North pole magnets may help release blockages and stimulate energy flow, promoting confidence and a sense of empowerment.

Benefits: Increases confidence, boosts self-esteem, and enhances the ability to assert one's personal power.

4. Heart Chakra (Anahata) and Magnet Therapy

Focus: Love, Compassion, Emotional Healing

The Heart Chakra governs love, compassion, and emotional

healing. Blockages here can lead to emotional pain, relationship issues, and difficulty experiencing love.

Magnet Therapy for Heart Chakra: Magnets placed on or around the chest area, near the Heart Chakra, can help release emotional blockages and promote love and compassion. South pole magnets are often used to enhance emotional healing and open the heart.

Benefits: Promotes emotional healing, fosters self-love and compassion, and encourages open-heartedness in relationships.

5. Throat Chakra (Vishuddha) and Magnet Therapy

Focus: Communication, Expression, Truth

The Throat Chakra is associated with self-expression, communication, and speaking one's truth. Blockages in this area can cause difficulty expressing oneself clearly or authentically.

Magnet Therapy for Throat Chakra: Magnets applied to the throat area or neck may help clear blockages in communication. North pole magnets can be used to facilitate the flow of energy, aiding in clear, truthful expression.

Benefits: Improves communication skills, enhances self-expression, and promotes speaking one's truth.

6. Third Eye Chakra (Ajna) and Magnet Therapy

Focus: Intuition, Insight, Mental Clarity

The Third Eye Chakra is related to intuition, perception, and inner vision. When blocked, it can lead to confusion, lack of direction, and difficulty trusting one's intuition.

Magnet Therapy for Third Eye Chakra: Magnets placed on the forehead, between the eyes (where the Third Eye is located), can help enhance clarity and intuitive abilities. North pole magnets are commonly used to stimulate energy flow in this area, clearing blockages and encouraging spiritual insight.

Benefits: Increases mental clarity, enhances intuition, and strengthens spiritual awareness.

7. Crown Chakra (Sahasrara) and Magnet Therapy

Focus: Spiritual Connection, Enlightenment

The Crown Chakra connects us to higher consciousness and the divine. Blockages here can create feelings of spiritual disconnection or a lack of purpose.

Magnet Therapy for Crown Chakra: Magnets placed on the top of the head or above the crown may help open the Crown Chakra and facilitate a deeper spiritual connection. South pole magnets are often used here to encourage the flow of energy and spiritual awareness.

Benefits: Enhances spiritual connection, promotes clarity and enlightenment, and strengthens the connection to universal consciousness.

Magnet Therapy Techniques for Chakra Healing:

Magnetic Pads or Patches: Special magnetic pads or patches can be placed on the body to directly affect the chakra points. These are often worn for extended periods to promote continuous energy flow.

Magnetic Jewelry: Magnetic bracelets, necklaces, and rings can be worn to help balance the body's energy field and stimulate specific chakras throughout the day.

Magnetic Therapy Mats: These mats contain embedded magnets and are often used for general energy healing or for specific chakra work, depending on the area of focus.

Hand-Held Magnets: Hand-held magnets can be used during a meditation or healing session to direct magnetic energy to specific chakra points.

Magnet Therapy and Chakra Healing: Considerations

Personal Sensitivity: Some individuals may be more sensitive to magnetic fields than others. It is important to start with mild intensity and observe how your body responds.

Consistency: Like any energy work, the benefits of magnet therapy are often cumulative. Regular use of magnetic therapy for chakra healing can enhance long-term results.

Integration with Other Practices: Magnet therapy works well in combination with other chakra healing practices, such as meditation, sound healing, or aromatherapy, to provide a more comprehensive approach to balancing and healing the chakra system.

NOTE: This method require professional help, not recommended for self-healing.

CHAPTER XLIV

CHAKRAS AND SOUND

Sound healing is a powerful and ancient practice that naturally aligns with the chakra system. Each chakra resonates with specific frequencies and sounds, which can be used to balance, open, or energize these energy centers.

Each chakra corresponds to a specific sound or vibration that can be used to stimulate and balance it.

1. Root Chakra (Muladhara)

Sound: "LAM" (Bija mantra)

Frequency: 256 Hz or 396 Hz

Instruments: Drums, low-frequency sounds (deep beats help grounding).

2. Sacral Chakra (Svadhisthana)

Sound: "VAM"

Frequency: 288 Hz or 417 Hz

Instruments: Flowing water sounds, bells, or smooth tones like singing bowls.

3. Solar Plexus Chakra (Manipura)

Sound: "RAM"

Frequency: 320 Hz or 528 Hz

Instruments: Chimes, brass instruments, or energizing gongs.

4. Heart Chakra (Anahata)

Sound: "YAM"

Frequency: 341 Hz or 639 Hz

Instruments: Harps, flutes, or harmonic tones that evoke love and compassion.

5. Throat Chakra (Vishuddha)

Sound: "HAM"

Frequency: 384 Hz or 741 Hz

Instruments: Wind instruments, vocal chanting, or harmonic singing bowls.

6. Third Eye Chakra (Ajna)

Sound: "OM" or "AUM"

Frequency: 426 Hz or 852 Hz

Instruments: Tuning forks, high-frequency sounds, or meditative chants.

7. Crown Chakra (Sahasrara)

Sound: Silent or "NG" or "OM" or "AUM"

Frequency: 480 Hz or 963 Hz

Instruments: Crystal singing bowls, silence, or meditative tones.

Tools for Chakra Sound Healing

Tuning Forks: These emit precise frequencies and can be placed near chakra points to restore balance.

Singing Bowls: Crystal or Tibetan singing bowls resonate with specific chakras based on their size and tuning.

Mantras: Chanting the bija mantras (LAM, VAM, RAM, etc.) activates and harmonizes each chakra.

Gongs: These create a full-spectrum sound that works on multiple chakras simultaneously.

Nature Sounds: Waterfalls, birdsong, and wind sounds can align with the energy of certain chakras (e.g., flowing water for the Sacral Chakra).

Practices to Align Chakras Using Sound

1. Chanting: Recite the bija mantra for each chakra during meditation.

Example: While meditating, chant "LAM" to focus on grounding the Root Chakra.

2. Listening to Solfeggio Frequencies: These healing frequencies align with chakras (e.g., 396 Hz for Root Chakra, 528 Hz for Solar Plexus Chakra).

3, Use headphones or speakers to listen during relaxation or sleep.

4. Sound Baths: Attend or create a sound bath session using singing bowls, chimes, and gongs to envelop yourself in vibrations.

5. Visualization with Sound: While meditating, pair chakra-specific sounds with visualization of their corresponding colors or

symbols.

Example Sound Healing Meditation for Chakras:

Set an Intention: Decide to bring balance to all chakras or focus on a specific one.

Choose a Sound: Play a recording, use an instrument, or chant the mantra.

Visualize and Breathe: Visualize the chakra's color and energy while breathing deeply.

Move Upward: Begin at the Root Chakra and work upward to the Crown Chakra, using the corresponding sounds and vibrations for each.

Note: Keep it simple, only practice, what you can practice comfortably.

CHAPTER XLV

CHAKRAS AND SELF ESTEEM

Chakras and Self-Esteem: Empowering Your Inner Strength

Self-esteem is the belief in your worth and abilities, forming the foundation for a confident and fulfilling life. The chakras, as energy centers in the body, are deeply connected to how we perceive ourselves. Each chakra influences specific aspects of self-esteem, from the security of the Root Chakra to the transcendence of the Crown Chakra.

By working with the chakras, we can heal wounds, release limiting beliefs, and build unshakable confidence in our authentic selves.

What is Self-Esteem?

Self-esteem encompasses:

Self-Worth: Recognizing your inherent value as a person.

Self-Respect: Setting boundaries and honoring your needs.

Self-Confidence: Trusting your ability to face challenges and succeed.

When the chakras are in balance, they collectively create a foundation for healthy self-esteem.

Imbalances, however, can lead to feelings of insecurity, self-doubt, or overcompensation.

1. Root Chakra (Muladhara): The Foundation of Worth

Theme: Safety and grounding.

Connection to Self-Esteem:

Provides a sense of belonging and security, essential for self-worth.

Supports the feeling that you have a right to exist and take up space.

Practices:

Visualize a red light at the base of your spine, grounding you in strength.

Repeat affirmations such as: "I am worthy of love."

Engage in grounding activities like walking barefoot on the earth.

2. Sacral Chakra (Svadhisthana): Emotional Authenticity

Theme: Creativity, emotions, and pleasure.

Connection to Self-Esteem:

Encourages acceptance of your emotions and the freedom to express them.

Boosts self-esteem by fostering joy and creative self-expression.

Practices:

Visualize a vibrant orange light flowing in your lower abdomen.

Engage in activities that spark creativity, like art, dance, or cooking.

Affirm: "I honor my feelings."

3. Solar Plexus Chakra (Manipura): The Powerhouse of Confidence

Theme: Personal power and self-esteem.

Connection to Self-Esteem:

Strengthens your ability to trust yourself and your decisions.

Encourages healthy boundaries and a strong sense of personal identity.

Practices:

Meditate on a golden light radiating from your solar plexus.

Practice yoga poses like Warrior Pose to embody confidence.

Affirm: "I am confident."

4. Heart Chakra (Anahata): Self-Love and Acceptance

Theme: Love and compassion.

Connection to Self-Esteem:

Encourages unconditional self-love and forgiveness.

Helps release feelings of inadequacy or self-judgment.

Practices:

Visualize a green or pink light expanding from your chest.

Practice loving-kindness meditation directed at yourself.

Affirm: "I accept myself as I am."

5. Throat Chakra (Vishuddha): Authentic Self-Expression

Theme: Communication and truth.

Connection to Self-Esteem:

Builds confidence in expressing your true self and asserting your needs.

Helps overcome fear of judgment or rejection.

Practices:

Chant the mantra "HAM" to activate your Throat Chakra.

Write or speak affirmations like: "I express my truth with courage."

Meditate on a blue light at your throat.

6. Third Eye Chakra (Ajna): Inner Clarity and Wisdom

Theme: Intuition and perception.

Connection to Self-Esteem:

Encourages trust in your intuition and inner guidance.

Promotes clarity about your purpose and direction in life.

Practices:

Visualize an indigo light at your Third Eye.

Practice mindfulness to detach from self-critical thoughts.

Affirm: "I trust my inner wisdom and see my true worth."

7. Crown Chakra (Sahasrara): Divine Connection

Theme: Transcendence and unity.

Connection to Self-Esteem:

Reminds you of your divine nature and infinite worth.

Transcends ego-based insecurities, aligning you with universal love.

Practices:

Meditate on a violet or white light above your head.

Practice gratitude for your existence as part of the cosmic whole.

Affirm: "I am an expression of divine love."

Common Chakra Imbalances and Their Effects on Self-Esteem

- Blocked Root Chakra:

Symptoms: Insecurity, fear, or feeling unsupported.

Impact: Difficulty establishing a sense of worth.

- Overactive Sacral Chakra:

  Symptoms: Overdependence on external validation.
  Impact: Inconsistent self-esteem.

- Underactive Solar Plexus Chakra:

  Symptoms: Lack of confidence, passivity, or self-doubt.
  Impact: Struggles with asserting yourself.

- Blocked Heart Chakra:

  Symptoms: Difficulty forgiving yourself or others.
  Impact: Lack of self-love and compassion.

- Blocked Throat Chakra:

  Symptoms: Fear of speaking up or self-censorship.
  Impact: Suppressed self-esteem.

- Blocked Third Eye Chakra:

  Symptoms: Confusion, doubt, or inability to trust intuition.
  Impact: Lack of clarity about your purpose and worth.

- Blocked Crown Chakra:

Symptoms: Disconnection from spirituality or feelings of isolation.

Impact: Lack of a higher sense of worth.

Holistic Practices to Boost Self-Esteem Through Chakras

1. Chakra Meditation: Focus on each chakra, visualizing its color and energy flowing freely.

2. Asana:

- Practice grounding poses for the Root Chakra, such as Mountain Pose.
- Use energizing poses for the Solar Plexus, like Boat Pose.
- Open the Heart Chakra with poses like Camel Pose.

3. Breathwork (Pranayama):

- Alternate Nostril Breathing for balance.
- Kapalabhati (Skull-Shining Breath) for confidence and empowerment.

4. Affirmations: Integrate chakra-specific affirmations into your daily routine.

5. Crystals: Work with stones like:

- Red Jasper for the Root Chakra.
- Citrine for the Solar Plexus Chakra.
- Rose Quartz for the Heart Chakra.

By aligning and balancing your chakras, you can unlock your true potential, transform insecurities, and step into a life of confidence and fulfillment. Self-esteem is not about perfection but about honoring your unique path and recognizing your infinite worth. When you embrace the energy of each chakra, you create a harmonious and empowered self that radiates authenticity, love, and resilience.

www.ingramcontent.com/pod-product-compliance
Lightning Source LLC
LaVergne TN
LVHW091305150826
845673LV00006B/1543

* 9 7 9 8 8 9 6 3 2 5 3 9 0 *